# THE B

*A POET'S MEMOIR THROUGH ...*

## CHETANA A.

INDIA · SINGAPORE · MALAYSIA

# Notion Press

Old No. 38, New No. 6
McNichols Road, Chetpet
Chennai - 600 031

First Published by Notion Press 2020
Copyright © Chetana A. 2020
All Rights Reserved.

ISBN 978-1-64892-973-1

*To*

*All the Versions that Were and Will be.*

# Contents

## II Connecting with Others

# III Providing Order

# IV Leaving a Mark

# Plausible Interpretations

# Foreword

Hi there,

So we finally meet here, in this moment of space and time. It never fails to surprise me, the way in which books and words teleport us the way they do.

An element of nature which may seem as a mere coincidence but exits for reasons that would unfold the mysteries of our very existence.

I have written my story in a hope that some day in some way I'll get to know yours too. For there is a reason why our eyes were meant to see others and not our selves.

I have been writing since I was 15 years old, and these poems span almost 17 years of my life. I always dreamt that one day I will be able to live my truth and publish a book of poetry, a part of me that could exist even when I ceased to do so.

Some have been lost here and there, but these are the ones I held on to or should I say they held onto me. When I started to get the manuscript ready and started to read all of the poems, especially the ones that were written ages ago, I felt very silly. For the girl or I think the 'Girls' I have been. I really was racking my brain as to how do I even begin to categorize them.

Then inspiration struck me with Carl Jung's work on Archetypes, the Swiss Psychiatrist and Psychoanalyst. It seemed perfect. It was a process that made me come to terms with all aspects of myself, the past, the present and the future. The lost girl didn't seem so foolish anymore.

It also made me realize that studying psychology and being a psychologist too is an integral part of me. I believed that each individual owns certain static traits; however, when I started categorizing the poems and reading about the archetypes, I realized that we possess all of these archetypes. At different points of our lives as we grow and experience circumstances and life.

Carl Jung, in his study, categorized the archetypes into four main subtypes based on people's motivations. The inherent yearning and seeking, the eternal need to connect with others at a higher level, the urge to find order and meaning in the things we experience and ultimately leaving a legacy and a mark on this world that we have existed which would remain even if we turn to ashes. Each of these four motivations have been further divided into what we call as archetypes, traits and universal characteristics and personas which are influenced by them. In all, there are 12 archetypes based on which I have categorized the poems, the underlying themes of the poems.

It's my sincere hope that you enjoy the poems as I am sharing with you a part of me that always brought me closer to the light in my journey this far. I hope it strikes something within you and allows you to feel and experience that we are all connected at a fundamental level even though our experiences may be unique and diversified. Therein the beauty of life lies...

Towards the end of the book, I have given plausible interpretations for each of my poems. This is the reason I have called it a memoir. The poems are still open to interpretation as the reader experiences them from their perspective. I hope you cherish the flavours as much as I have enjoyed brewing them.

# I

# YEARNING AND SEEKING

# The Innocent

*"I see the hope dimming in your eyes, and I can't wait to show you a world filled with all the things that can go right,*

*Fiercely I believe in all the goodness in a heart, for paradise is meant for people like us,*

*Mistakes are something that I often worry about,*

*It would be naive of me to be in the wrong.*

*All I need is some faith and optimism to build a world which always has happy endings."*

# The Beauty of Beauty

Innocence we feel is

The beauty of all

But when you know

Of the seen and call,

"Would have I had not seen

Such a scene,

I could have been in

A heaven of beauty,

And happily, then I would

Have lived, rather

Being in this duty unclean."

But remaining beautiful

After knowing it all

Is the beauty of it all.

# Wild Child

Not very proud of what I do sometimes

Not very proud of how I feel...

Trying trying it's hard to wait

What do I say to myself when I grow faint...?

I am strong is all that I can say.

So weary and tired I grow, trying

To make sense of the things, I feel I should know,

Wanting things my heart sets to

But knowing life is like a child

Who is creative, curious and can never be told...

How do I tame this wild child in me...

It would be great if we could turn a leaf new each day,

But unless a leaf fulfils its purpose, it can't be shed away,

So, I wait now figuring out what all these leaves in my head mean,

My heart and head throb at the thought of all these things,

So, I guess I should now just close my eyes and think about

All the exams I have to pass…

Or then just close my eyes and know…

This phase, I must pass to take a new stance.

# Tears

It tears up my heart to be so cold,

It tears up my heart to see tears

In the things I mould.

With so much care, I try to hold

Onto the things I have got,

To avoid disappearing of things I love.

To me, they are much more than just

Parts of the world,

But they are to me my own.

It pierces my heart

With a thousand knives to see

My own blood rises up to their own.

They try their least to make things
work.

And it tears up my heart to see
them so.

# It Feels as If

It feels as if the ship seems to be disappearing in the quicksands of time...

Nothing is going to stay the same anymore,

The winds of change can be ghastly and wrenching...

Those who were meant to be the world, Were the first ones to leave,

All they left was a rope, I wonder if it was for me to hang myself in or to pull me out.

Love lost its meaning, all that seems left is an empty shell,

The turtle that hatched seems to have slowed down all the healing tides.

Can't trust the ones close to you,

To guard your heart with fervour, they seem to have created twin towers,

Double standards to fool you into thinking that

They gave you their heart when they took yours...

And now your left in the moat,

With the heavy, shiny armour that once the knight carried.

Knowing that that's all you have, to fight off

The crocodiles trying to bite a piece out of you.

Still unsure if the broken pieces are a boon or a blessing, would they complete a puzzle or are they shards of glass waiting to cut open.

These are the tests of time, I want to believe.

True love, if it exists, would surpass all of this,

But I guess I am naive; it always takes two for love to survive.

Happily ever after's seem good only in books,

When you wake up each day without an embrace,

Then you realise realities are made of giggles that show the promise of happiness but turn out to be nothing but futile introspection.

# Why so Serious

He had asked her, is this a little too much...

After a verse where he told her what it felt with an intensity of the Sun...

Too weak to speak, as blood ran down her feet,

That moment she had waited for a long time...

All she could do was say, wait till the dawn of light,

Then I'll make all your wishes come alive...

And when the day did come,

It turned out that the dream had changed into a pragmatic eulogy...

Now when she thinks back,

With the innocence of a curiosity filled child,

There is so much more she would have liked to say,

There are so many pages she wants to write that mills and boons would not suffice...

He has no idea, of her mind and souls calibrating scales...

So, lost he is in his own sacrifice,

That nothing compares in atoning smiles...

Whatever may be the case,

She was about to go back and join the garden in the Mad Hatters way,

But just then she pulled back from the rabbit hole,

For now, she knew how to put an end to the jabberwocky

In her head that made her demons grow...

It doesn't take much, once the night has cleared;

Just need to minus the selfishness, from the love and passion...

And there you had it, a brilliant amalgamation,

Of what it is to accept your destiny,

It's ok to not say anything,

Just gulp the hiccup down if you want to save yourself from splitting a beat...

A story as beautiful as any,

For, after all, life is not to be taken too seriously.

# Love

Who can define the beautiful world?

They shall be immortal forever they shall!

For it is this world that connects every

Soul, for this, is what makes

Everything that is so pure and strong,

In love, they are the moon and the earth, in love

They are the lovers who need no thing...

Four letters are too small too lame to explore

Its horizon for it is made of so many dawns.

# Seed to a Tree

Your missing me aren't you...

Can't say it... How can you?

If you do, your honour would be at stake,

If you don't, then you have a fear of losing me again...

What would you do...

So you throw a pebble at me,

To catch my attention...

You know you have missed all that

Loving admiration...

So when I do look back,

You scratch your head with that

Silly boy style,

Pretending that it wasn't you

Who threw it all this while...

Do I say to you, my

Little child,

You need to grow up

And quit all these riddles,

Your pebbles make it difficult,

And I can't walk on bubbles.

You know I have done all I could,

There is nothing more that I can give...

It's your wishes and prayers that

Have kept me lonely all this while,

But soon the time will come,

And I won't have a chance to

Tell you

That I am here, don't you cry...

So it's time you know that everything will be just fine...

Now set yourself free and don't Fear to fly...

No more can I give unless I receive,

For that is how

This world was made to grow from a seed to a tree.

# Strength Within

At night when you are lonely

And scared of being alone,

Fear not for evil can do you no harm,

No monster can tear you apart,

No ghost can drown within you,

But only if you are scared of them

Only if you fear death

They will be able to harm you or cast a spell.

But if you fear no one

Only then

You can breathe freely.

Within you, you will find

All the faith you will ever need;

You will see that you need no one to

Stand beside you for you have the

Strength to stand beside someone else.

# The Philosopher

"I see you so lost and I can't help but intervene, to help you understand the mysteries I have uncovered in my vagaries.

Wisdom is the treasure I seek as I delve inward; all the nourishment I need is in intellectual stimulation. I abhor the ones who misguide and deceive; They will never taste the freedom that truth unfolds.

I look at the heavens, preoccupied with details of how it all works, with me they share stories untold. It's the truth that sets my soul on fire, as bright as the stars that constellations hold."

# Phases

It all starts with one breath

The day you enter this perishable beautiful

World filled with change, you didn't know then,

You don't know now and neither will you know

What will lie ahead

You see, listen, feel and learn to understand

What according to others is right or wrong,

You don't know then that you will have to think for
Yourself ahead.

Care and attention love and desire is what

You seek next to help you feel appreciated

You start to change with goodness if all is well

Or then hurt if you are taught the hard way,

You don't know then that this might change you
forever...

That age comes when they say you are stubborn,
strong-headed,

Difficult but you feel how could the ones who told you
always

To do the right things can be so imperfect and

Still say they have done right,

you don't know then that Later you will have to learn to control yourself as

You realise everyone makes mistakes...

You learn to explore, think and discover,

You realise you need that special someone

To be there with you as you grow body mind and soul,

You don't know then that the plans you made

May not work out as you had wanted them too

But you will know better things lie ahead

If you have the strength to stand up again...

You then try to mould others the way which would Please you,

So that you can feel secure, you want to

Take over your little world now,

But you don't know then It's not that easy to be a king for each person is

A hero in their own life, so you adjust and try

To find a dream that will contain all your desires

And the ones who will help you to fulfil them...

You make your choices, you stumble, and you fall,

You hate yourself sometimes,

You hate the world the rest of the time, nothing seems fair...

But you need to know then that

Responsibilities will make you stronger,

You need to stand up for what you believe,

Forgiveness will help you go forward,

Forgiving yourself will

Make you heal,

With fairness is not how this world was made

But it is made up of you and me who

Can give it the shape of our dreams...

# The Catalyst

The day I met you my world was going to change,

It was going to be a ride I could never be able to forget.

Every time you came beside me, I could not move away,

The strength of your magic pulled me your way.

The look in your eyes told me you would stay,

But now my heart will never be the same.

You came to me as the water of a river

And quenched my thirst before you led me your way.

You guided me with the perfect advice,

You loved me with the perfect spice,

The strength you gave me, the care you showered upon me,

The companion you became for me, no one can ever do

That for me, I feel.

Every song I hear reminds me of you,

Arousing the passion that makes me love you.

Accepting me as I was, making me the way I am,

You became my strength when I needed you,

You became My sword when I wanted you.

Showing a beautiful world, you made me trust you,

But when I woke up, this world was not true.

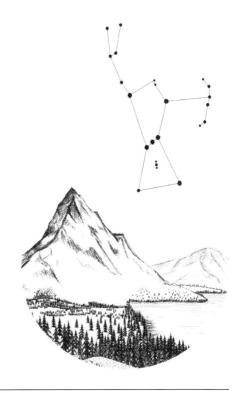

# Meanings

Even if my voice falters,

Even if my deeds seem weak,

Even if my ears miss a beat,

Or even if my eyes close,

Nothing of it would change this moment,

For in this moment I have loved you with all my heart,

So much so that even if you believe me or not,

My love for you will still shine,

If just you would say, you want to be mine...

I know you want no fight, I know you want no barriers or mights,

I know you don't want troubled waters to sail on,

Nor words that would put a stain on,

You don't want any adventures...

I know that because you see me as your home

Not a hunt that brings out your worst...

Instead just a soft pillow, that will bring you soothing dreams...

Am still thinking why my love said I don't love him,

What should I say, what should I do to make him feel special...?

I know his tantrums, I know his ways,

He says those words only to

Let me know that he needs my pampering,

That he needs my attention...

Would a shower of my kisses make his heart melt?

Would the touch of my hand let him know that am his?

Or just the thought of me holding him would let my love know,

How much he means to me...

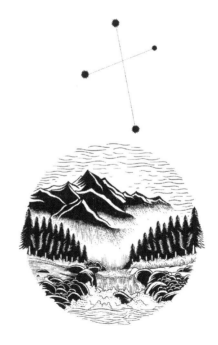

# Mirrors

Words when expressed

Are sometimes reflections of you

In the mirrors of others eyes...

The mirror will always reflect back what it sees...

Darkness will blind both,

Light will shine twice as bright...

But how do you erase an image

Cast wrong...

You try to adjust the mirror for yourself...

You change your ways for other's sake...

You look into a mirror made of glass

Which will not just show
you,

But a new world behind
that glass...

Or then you just feel

There is no need to look
anymore...

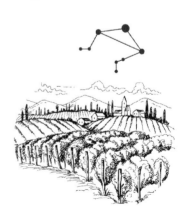

# Something's

Everyone teaches you so many things,

So many words so many rules,

Some teach you how you should be

Some show you who you should believe,

Some tell you what you must do,

Some ask you to follow in their steps.

Each day you live for others,

Each day you miss something.

One day then comes when

Everyone who cared

Don't care who you are anymore

And seem to still want to change you

Into something that you're not.

You try then to be yourself

Standing up for what you have missed,

But it still hurts to see them disappointed

As you haven't turned into what

They wanted to.

What are you to do now,

It feels so hard for you to go on,

How dark the days have become,

No one taught you how to be by yourself.

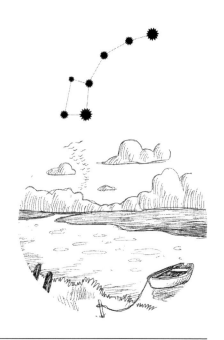

# Fear

The dream that I had that night
Will remain with me forever,
Making me realise the facts of life
Waking me up to bright new light.
For the dream I had was of death
For the truth I realised was of faith
Whether I will remain as I am or
Whether I will fade to a new star.
Losing myself from the things I know
Was the fear I awaked, from a dream
I thought I very well knew;
Like the mist, it crept over me
Covering me with a fear unknown
But the truth of light it showed me by life
For the things that go, make way for

The things that come

And death will turn into

The beginning of a Sun.

# The Chord

In the search to find a method to the madness

It is possible to stumble and fall to relentless darkness...

But when you kindle the light, the wick and wax has to melt,

The dark core burns as the flame flickers...

The smile and frown,

A part of the same set of lips...

Which forms the Cupid's bow...

Either way, others see you lose your marbles,

Even when you show courage, despite the hardships...

When two eyes can't see one,

Imagine the chaos that it causes, to the I'll devised mind,

Do you push the incongruence away,

Or do you pull in and understand

The kaleidoscope through which

They have shaped their gaze...

You say black, I say grey,

None of them truly colours...

Then why the sand storms,

Why the glaciers avalanche...

It's so difficult to let things be...

The need for that umbilical cord,

Seems so primitive,

But yet it forces you to look for

Bonds that go beyond comprehension...

Best is to lay your mind to sleep,

It has travelled enough portals

To last more than a lifetime...

The sweetness of harmony can be felt

Only when one loses themselves

To the chaos that justifies the archetype...

# Bones of Contention

Don't hate me for being too harsh...

Tell me, is it my fault...

Tell me where have I gone wrong...Is it me who has been blocking your path?

Have I ever wished ill, that you can mock...

Has there been any dereliction on my part,

Have I not done enough to help you find a cure to your ailing heart...

Have I not done everything that you have asked...

Is it my fault if happiness hasn't come in your days?

Or is it yourself standing in your own way...

Am I culpable in not getting what you want,

Have I stood in the doorway or barricaded the boulevard that you claim that I don't allow anyone else to reach your shore...

Can you convict me only because I tried to do what was requisite,

Haven't you been doing the same and

I am still happy even if there have been bones of contention.

So let's not disquiet about the meanderings of life,

For one can't swim against the tide...

But take delight in the simplicity of the wind beneath the flight...

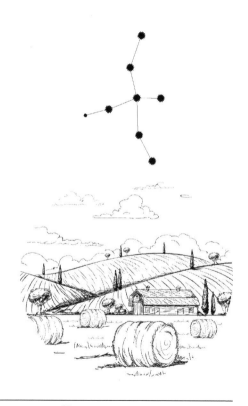

# A Path Different

Sinful you are if you

Hurt someone,

A sin you have committed if you

Harmed anyone.

But this can be made

Right if you correct the wrong

And help someone who

You have done so wrong.

What anyone says cannot

Always be right, it is up

To you to fly your own kite.

If for you something is not wrong,

Then it does not mean

That you have to do that something

Once more.

You are free to do what you want

Not necessarily be what you do

Has to be right or wrong.

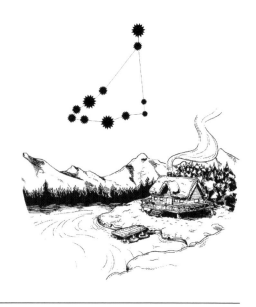

# Infinity

I listen to the melodies

And the sky becomes my canvas...

A colossal portrait of you

Painted in the hues of evening

Spanning, vastly as if enveloping the

Whole atmosphere as much as my eyes can take...

A divine moment when I know

This image surpasses all the

Ifs, buts and fears...

Only if you would have asked the question

Yet again, the summer would have given

You another answer...

I was stronger when your eyes fell on me,

The iron birds reminding I could fly

No matter the burdens...

You should have asked and the answer

Would have been different...

Did leave it all, but you refused yet again...

Now am in the valley,

My strength weakens here,

A constant reminder that I can't leave

The hand of the one who caught it,

When I had no one, not even you...

The rains are here again,

But am still barren,

Still shedding tears of blood,

Absence of a child that could

Seal or break the bonds that there are...

I still feel, maybe it's not too late,

I know you need me to make a move,

And I need you to do the same...

And here is where the time stays still...

Where Vienna calls out to me,

And I tell myself, no more,

I have tried very hard,

But this time let destiny take its course,

It's easier then, it feels right then...

Maybe I'm wrong... maybe I'm right...

But I'm ok with whatever be the plight...

I just need to know if you're alright...

And the rest will be sealed by the letters

Written to Infinity...

# Intensely Same

We fight to see whose wounds are deep,

Is it you who has suffered more?

That's not possible we tell ourselves,

For how it can be, that someone else's agony

Can be greater than our own despair...

A child comes with a cut finger, another with a broken arm,

To the observer, the broken arm seems graver,

But for a mother, the pain of both is all but the same...

That is how simple it is, there is no greater or smaller in misery,

We all fall with the same intensity...

Some of us make a stride within a week,

Some take a fortnight,

Years pass by, and still, we hold on to the scars,

Reminding us of how brave we were...

We tell others of how strong we have been,

Some tell a different story,

They say how unfair the world has been,

Without realising, they have the power to heal any indignity...

You and I are but the same,

Stronger than diamonds but as fragile as slate...

# The Worship

The part of myself,

As beautiful as me,

But like a flickering tube light,

It made me unsure if I saw things right,

The journey of contemplation,

An obsession to deny the feelings

Of overwhelming puzzles,

Not one or two but they came

In the company of dozens,

Like the extended family

That pulls and pricks at your

Dreams and desires, reliving my childhood,

In the kitchen a subservient lonely wife,

The outdoors the escape from the battles raging within the bedroom,

The living room the portal where I met

Those who were new as well as the cartoons,

The darkness of the bedroom is where the

Fairy tales stemmed from the anxious chest,

The show of the pure and profane was housed

In the cold tiles of the smallest room

Played by the characters of disgust and shame,

The room of faith is where

The ropes of abandonment would dance,

However, the flame showing hope that

Turned into the most practical of minds,

Where prayers would never consist asks.

Forcing myself to write, to concentrate,

To make sense of the things around me,

Taking its toll on me,

Reminding myself that nothing comes easy,

And I deserve no happiness without

Some excruciating realities.

The irritation of the scratching paws,

The Unmelodious temple chants,

The white light making the retina strained,

The music unduly playing the rhythms I don't like

A distorted reality which is in front of me,

Mocking me, inadequacy dripping on my

Intellectual audacities,

My voice is lost,

So I borrowed the one of an angel that turned into a bully,

Idolising it, trusting it to guide me,

Hoping to protect me from the pervert that

I was warned about who would take away

My innocence.

Turned my thinking into the extremes of black and white,

Idolising and then demeaning that

Didn't come up to my expectations.

The hypocrisy, cowardliness and lack of awareness

Of the loves that transpired due to the

Borderline uncertainties that wiped off the smile and

Made humour something to be taken personally.

The desperate need to make up for the profound loss,

To find someone to replace the love once I had,

Torn always between two sides of the war,

Swimming in the sea of guilt for not being able to choose a team,

The dissociation is the only method to feel whole again.

The passive style of talking would build up to resentment,

The anxious-avoidant attachment

causing the flight and fight response.

Trying till it gives me the restless arm and legs response

Where I feel I just want all of this to stop now.

So, I try to encompass all the concepts into one,

And form a belief that there is unconditional love,

No idol worship but different levels of consciousness,

A collective of all that I have understood through my senses.

Still doubting and distrustful of myself and the faith,

Trying to relate to how others find their ways,

The rituals are minimised to acts of love,

The holy book with empathetic conversations,

The spirituality remains as it is,

The stories of grandeur are filled with fantasy.

It takes time to come out of the trance,

But time will only tell if I am on the right path,

The uncertainties are many but at least am learning

To integrate me from the fractures that have been eluding me.

The fear of loss and distrust follows me like a shadow,

But hoping to make friends with it as it is

What is created when light is shed on you.

Am I 'special', is the question

I have believed in, without knowing the answer,

Well, it's my story, and I think I can tell it in any way that I like.

A new beginning,

An umpteenth chance,

The disappointments that followed through the

Impatience and compulsive tasks.

I have been trying to find,

Alternative responses,

This journey, however, has a whole range of emotions

That I don't always comprehend.

So this is an ode to myself,

Hoping I find others who one day would

Understand what it is that I am saying.

For, for me happiness is only one thing,

Finding people who have similar wavelengths like me.

# Bruises Blue and Black

I want to know...

I want to know what it is that you have given up...

I want to hear the cries of your soul that you have muffled up...

Hold the tears, down in my palms, and watch,

What makes you so sad all the while...

I want to know the scars that you hide,

But still show what you have engraved with

Flowers placed on the verge of your might...

What it is that you are so bitter about...

What promises have you made to yourself,

That brings you down to the depths of the earth...

You think I am blind, that I still haven't placed the puzzles in my mind...

I know each screech, I know the bruises made of blue and black,

I have held your hand through it all...

I know you have fallen with a thousand broken smiles...

So what? So what? Even gods were made to fall...

How long will you keep using it to make more corpses,

Don't you know by now the promises made

To the dead can be broken for

They are free from this world,

In a place where they can finally be together

Without worrying about the happiness of their loved ones,

For that's all that they want...

A smile, a smile on your face...

Who are you trying to prove to, what are you trying to prove...

If it is for others then just forget it,

Time is too precious to waste it...

If it is to me, I already know every alphabet and syllable...

I should be the one mocking at the world's plight,

But still, happily, I truly believe that life

Has been kind, and I know what pulls you,

And it's not gravity but a memory that is

The Centre of your universe...

So, it's difficult to bear the rotations,

But the more you will pay attention,

You will realise there is no room for attribution,

So shed your skin, into the dusk at the horizon,

No more pain will I let you bear than

What you have already been through...

You need to believe that you can find that contentment...

No point blaming others or yourself for holding you back

As the grains of sand can never be told what is to be done...

Tell me honestly, hasn't it become

A little bit easier since the break of dawn,

Since the shadows came out of the light...

So breathe in the freedom and let the memories fall,

For there has never been a better beginning to

Make friends and do away with woes.

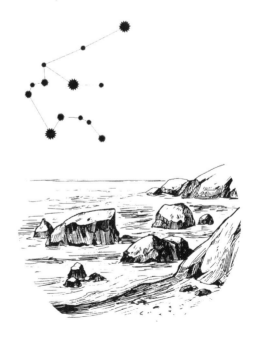

# Embers Red

No one deserves the pain

None happiness...

Perfection is the line drawn

Between empathy and arrogance...

What will you take with you, When you draw your last
breath...

Your finest gold chains or your shoes and lace...

Will, it be your friends or the one you love,

Is it your soul or the experiences that you hold...

If you think you can choose...

It's better to laugh at your own joke...

For none of it would be weightless,

And death doesn't carry any burdens...

It sets you free, that's why the line is drawn...

It liberates the one to cast its shell...

Hell is left for all those who are left at the

Embers red...

You laugh, you cry, waiting for someone to hear...

Prayers turn into answers when you

Stop waiting for miracles to happen...

# Now

In the end no matter how many ways

You devise to protect the self,

You would never be successful in stopping

Yourself from getting extinguished,

No matter how much you try to understand,

The dimensions would always be infinite.

You can try and find one equation that fits it all,

But there will always be new frontiers that

Will require a reshuffling of the things you know.

What purpose is then left,

But to accept what all that is you are Now.

# The Explorer

"I see your wings descending, and I can't help but implore
you to seek an adventure to quench your wonder,

Being true to one's self is the fierceness I carry within.

I am the force of nature that refuses to be caged, even if I
am tagged a misfit by the trapped conformists.

To find meaning to my existence,

I surf through the tides of time and space, A wanderer I am
who is on a holy quest."

# Sky Life

Darker than red
Darker than blue
Darker than black
A star still shines in you.

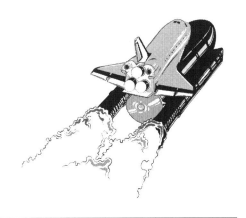

# Youth

The creases on your shirt get ironed out,

The folds in the curtain straighten when you pull,

Those creases on your forehead

Make a hot iron of your mind,

The folds in your life, straighten

Your thinking, quite a bit.

The Butterfly Effect makes you

Wonder of your own effect,

Should you walk on a given

Path or create your own...

But when youth matures, it realises,

The given trajectory, equals to, grand destiny,

Your own way, equals to, your own destiny,

Like mathematics? You would love life,

Variables dancing around trying to find,

Infinite solutions to finite problems,

Practice makes perfect,Twelve hours to solve the waking,

Twelve hours to answer the awakening...

Integration you see was not my expertise,

BODMAS is all that I can remember

Bridging, Occupation, Destiny, Meaning, Asserting, Self,

Equals to youth,

YOU...TH...Thinking was that word,

This was lost while writing TH...

# A New Beginning

So much we try we still can't make things right,

Can't seem to smile now when

you know you can't trust yourself anymore,

So many realisations so many lessons learnt,

But they still won't help you

To get back to where you were

Nor to where you want to go,

A silver lining a new season

A new beginning that is all

That is left to hope for now...

# Skin Deep

Happiness lies within the heart

No one can tell whether it's there or not

It has only a warm feeling within

Sadness lies deep within

Beneath the skin deep in the heart

No one can share no one can bear

The piercing pain caused by the heart...

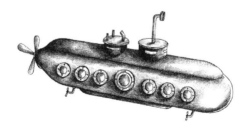

# Freedom

Why do you want to care
In this world of yours,
If all that surrounds you is
Just yourself and no one,
You can make it happen
Whatever it may be,
Just close your eyes
And see all that you need.
Make things happen with
Things you can change
And no need to worry
For something that cannot be changed,
Cause they need, not you,
But someone else,
So why bother to wreck your
Self when there are so
Many things that you
Surely can change.
Heaven is it if you want

For yourself, or is it

Someone's love that

You want to share?

Whatever it may be,

You can have it all,

Only if you,

Let yourself free.

Why do you want to

Depend on someone

Or something,

To make you happy,

If it is you, who is to be made

Happy.

It can't be that bad,

The way which you have chosen,

If all it does is makes you satisfied.

# A Poem

I dreamt a beautiful dream

Standing now in front of thee

Fates entwined

No matter what

I'll still breathe the divine

A change

A cause

A purpose

To live the life

You were made for

Through the recesses of your mind

You uncover the truths

Pulling you behind

Setting yourself free

To believe what you

Were meant to be

An epic, a poem, a dream

A fire that would

Kindle other souls

This is what you are

This is what you were meant to be

A mystery looking for the stars

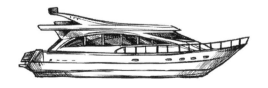

# Discover

Above the mountains or in the sea
I see some holy scene,
The face of my beloved is it so bright or
Is it a bird with flying wings;
What beauty is that makes me wonder
Am I a part of this magical wonder.
What other treasures does this
Incredible land hold or does it hide
Some fears untold.
Why can't I just feel happy and fly
Like the eagles high above.
I am a wonder in myself; I think,
Waiting to be discovered by someone
Like me.

# Whole

Two friends, one looking

At the night sky

And the other at the

Dark Ocean and knowing

They can't see the horizon anymore.

# The Rose

Masters protect the
Secrets of Mortals,
Through metaphors and codes.
Sacred rituals of love
Have been formed for the
Secret of this creative magic.
Simple is the key, to this
Secret, divine proportion and
So many other mysteries,
Just as there are many
Paths for one cause to be seen.
They are all around you, the keys
That open one door;
But only those who deserve
Shall see the light.

# I Am

Never-ending I am

Like the stars in the sky

The water in the seas

The seasons of a year

Like the leaves on a tree.

Unique like everyone

Strong like everything

I am.

I am the vision that I see

I am the sound that I hear

I am the touch that I feel

I am the voice that I sing,

Who can define me are people who

Do not know

Who cannot understand me are people

Who I don't know.

Forever will it be

I may never know

For everything is a mystery,

An ending story.

I am the star, I am the drop

I am the seasons, I am the leaves;

Definite in certain ways

Which make them what they are

But different for all the ways that are.

Note: '*This poem was broadcasted on BBC Ireland radio on 16th Oct 2014.'

# II

# CONNECTING WITH OTHERS

# The Orphan

"I see you there cast aside, and I can't help but be sincere in holding out my hand,

All are created equal is what I believe fiercely; a sense of belonging is what gives meaning to destiny.

I would do anything to fit in, as long as it relies on virtues of simplicity for, I fear to lose my self over superficial relationships.

I have trekked far and wide, to find my tribe,

Come walk with me, right here by my side."

# Wonders Within

Fairies and angels

Wings with which

They all can fly,

Are they really true,

I wonder why?

But now I get it

For the lands of fairies

Is the way...?

For they make us feel

So calm and happy

As if we are one of them.

It is the way that leads

To our hearts and then

Leads us to think that,

There can be more to us.

We are the angles

That we believe are true,

It is the feeling

That we have around them

That makes us wonder,

We need to look

For someone like them.

Anything can be true

In this world of ours

Cause it's of

Wonders that made us cross.

Note: '*This poem won special recognition in an online international poetry competition in 2004.'

# The Candescent Zephyr

I can still go weak in my knees

If only you say, Yes, please...

You are the pivot of the daydreams...

You're there even in the night themes...

Inspiring me into candescent imaginative streams...

You know I can read your mind,

Catch that skipped heartbeat when

The flash smiles,

The roots that go deep within,

You know buried within the soil,

They only get tougher to find the

Sunshine...

The marriage of two minds isn't a

Mirage but the reality of the divine...

You won't approve of the things I say

But I know you have me as your wallpaper

May it be night or day...

These words just a reminder, that love

Still transcends all desires...

The embers still singing to the zephyr...

And that's why you shall never hear me

Banter, for I, have loved you from the day

You said ...

To yourself... I do...

I knew...

# Killing Myself Softly

Things I have to do
To make others happy
By killing myself softly.
I don't have to do them
I know I don't
But I do choose to do them
I don't know why.
It gives them happiness
And me a whole new
Experience, that is why
I think I do things
That kills me softly.

# Driving Loneliness

The only way to
Drive your loneliness away
Is to be with the people
Who you love,
But don't you get sad if no
Ones there
Cause you can still bloom
By doing the things you love,
If you can't think of anything
Then, it will be my pleasure
To show you how wonderful this
World can be.
You can either read a book or watch
A movie or you can just sit back and
Watch yourself do the things you can't
When you are awake or too busy to
Give yourself time.
If that my friend isn't what you are

Then you can just go out and see

The world goes by or you can

Sing some melody tune and help

Someone to make you happy.

# Sold my Soul

The nervousness wrecks my soul

Don't you know I too feel scared?

Like a little girl afraid of ghosts...

But Still, you tease me

Knowing everything that there is to know...

Spare me the puzzles,

I have no answers to the snakes and ladders...

My mind ceases to contemplate

All the permutations and combinations...

Do you want to hear me say,

That let's not meet again,

Let's go our separate ways...

But I know the whispers

You want in your ears...

Only if you knew what it costs me

To write each syllable ...

But still, I do, thinking it might bring

A smile to your heart when

You say you feel nothing more...

But why is it that your face lights up

The moment you see me...

Only if he had the humility to accept

What he is receiving,

Without questioning and

Asking more of me...

But I have given all I can provide,

For I sold my soul

For a lifetime of memories...

# See You Again

She wakes up with a smile on her face...

Feeling surprised by the bulb lighting in her head...

Why hadn't she thought about this earlier,

That she could meet him sooner...

What a beautiful story to tell...

So, she decides to write him a letter...

Too nervous to speak,

What if dishonourably he hurts her,

The words always running out of his grip,

But finally, he agrees to have a meeting...

As they walk across the pathway,

Taking in the summer days,

But somehow trying to encompass

All that is walking their way...

Just one name, and it pulls you to the center of the universe,

Time seems to go slow,

It's been too long since snow...

They try to shake hands but somehow it doesn't seem to blend,

A hug is more appropriate for each know,

That it has been a long way...

Finally sitting across the bench,

Still trying to gather all that is left,

How are you?

Seems such an excellent disguise to start somewhere...

Who would have thought that within a minute?

All the awkwardness would dry away...

It was nothing as they had imagined but

Something so much more than they envisioned...

Not in the, I want to steal a kiss malady,

But I just want to see you warmly sort of way...

All the masks falling down, like the winter leaves,

The beauty of a bare Deciduous tree...

All the strings of attachment just fall,

To weave a stronger bond,

Not that of which ties you down but

Of which Kites can fly as much as they want...

He did always ask her,

Why was she so kind to him?

She said ...

That is all she knows how to be with him...

Not to hold him back or stop him in his track,

But because he is after all the boy

Whose will she has awed by...

It was her turn now to get the answers,

Why would he always be so mean and

Then cause disasters...

So, he told her, that's how it had to be;

Otherwise, the affections would have been too evident,

And that's the only way he knew to save their dignity...

They smiled at each other and then up at the sky,

What lovely hues it had turned, forgetting all the despair...

Life's ironies had been the funniest jokes,

The pain clenching agony that had washed away their hopes...

But now, sitting under the same sky, none mattered;

For now, the dice had

Been rolled in favour of their fates...

It didn't matter if they parted ways,

No more did it matter if words weren't exchanged,

There was this faith that as long as the stars would navigate,

They always dared to climb mountains

Higher than Everest...

Then again maybe they would meet,

And talk about their fascinating journey,

Still checking on the spider silk bonds that

Would withstand the distance of a galaxy...

Free they were to make new alliances,

Find different worlds that would put a smile on their face...

Finally, they accept each other with all their masquerades...

And when the time came to say goodbye,

All they both said in an instance was...

See you again, somewhere somehow.

# My Ally

A school day it was when I met you

Came right by and just sat next to you,

Later you told how funny you felt

With me coming and reading your book.

It was a day which was meant to

Be remembered by not only me but also you.

Sharing our tiffin's laughing with our friends

We did do that when we were in school

But it would be more fun when

We spoke on the phone,

For secrets were to be shared

Only between me and you.

It would be a very long list if I started with

What all we have shared but I won't stop here

Cause I have to tell my friend;

"Our friendship is true because we know

We still our together and I will be there

For you, if you need me ever or never.

I cannot define what it's that I see in

You which makes me feel so close to you

But I know one thing that I am sure of,

That I like the way you are and ask you

To always be my friend forevermore.

# The Jester

*"I see your frown and all I want is, for those lips to curl into the widest of grins. Come now, put on the masquerade and join me for a dance.*

*I fiercely believe that laughter is the best medicine; the pure joy of living in the moment has proven to be the doorway to even enlightenment.*

*So don't judge me to be too frivolous, I don't waste time; for I know the importance of comical timing. I would die of boredom if I didn't have a trick up my sleeve; eventually, you learn to juggle, if you have been living twenty thousand leagues under the sea."*

# Crush

Butterflies in my stomach

I can feel when you pass by me

My heart starts to race

When our eyes meet

Looking at you has to be done

In secret cause this game that I am playing

Can make me lose everything,

Saying

"For why did I look at the face so charming?

And make a fool of myself so very easily".

# Neon Sign

Say something...

Send me a signal

That you're feeling the same thing...

It's like the weather...

When the storm comes,

There is no Stopping it...

A calm just before the storm...

That's how it feels when you

Dropdown your guards...

I wish you knew, I secretly hope,

That you let down your defences,

Maybe just once in a while...

It's crazy patience, not knowing,

Would it be you or I who would,

Lose this fight only to come closer...

Please keep your rationalities to the side,

Can't you see am restless like a kite,

Tug the thread to your left,

That's where your heart is still kept,

For me to delve into,

No matter how hard you try to not show...

What more do you want me to say,

You would have known all this if

You weren't as slow as a tube light...

# Forbidden Love

What you do to me is not fair...

The games that you play,

You make it too hard for me to care...

But still, my heart now plays in this mist

Of forbidden play...

You rob me of myself,

You steal the peace of my heart...

But I still don't know why

I am drawn to this sin of forbidden love...

If you are the weather of this earth

I am the sky, in which you tread,

I bring you within me and

You are the one who fills

The seasons within me...

I know how special you are,

I have always told you

How you complete me...

But you did choose to let me go...

That I can never make it right...

# Beauty and the Beast

And the beauty said to the beast...

So what if your face is imperfect,

Do you think one should judge the book by its cover...

Do you believe eyes are all that important...

I see you for who you are...

Others should see you for who you are...

Do you think I did not notice...

Just because I didn't bring it to your notice...

One small one big,

So many frames I was bound to realize...

One to see the world,

The other like the pirates who use it for night vision...

Did you not know?

Beauty lies in the eyes of the beholder...

Imperfections are what make you just perfect, and the world will see...

Through your eyes alone...

So such trifling things don't bother me...

Get over yourself and put on some music...

There are plenty of damsels waiting...

My work is done here...

So now you can be in peace.

# The Mango Tree

We love like fools,
Expecting everything from one soul,
Then reality strikes like thunder,
Changing the definition of amour.
The waves of contentment,
Ripple through the veins of time,
It's not always that you can do the
Right thing, every single time...
It's like the need to blow soap
Bubbles into the air,
Creating floating small worlds of our own,
Though all grown up, we still like to play.
The games aren't played in the field anymore,
Nature, players and arena have changed...
But the innocence in them can be seen,
When the intentions are clean...
Wasn't hide and seek one of your favourites?
That's why the silly rush still exists ...
But it doesn't mean we don't go back

To our homes when the night falls,

It doesn't mean we don't make plans to meet again,

For another day of pretend play...

We can choose to be whoever we want,

Without being judged for the laughter,

Crying and craziness that ensued in the game...

How I miss those days where I ran bare feet,

Without a care in the world of how I should feel...

Mortal enemies for only a day if it was Katti,

Forgiven the next day easily if it was Batti.

No one likes to play games with

Those simple rules anymore...

Now we want fancy words and deeds

To cover our butts of embarrassment...

Forgetting the joy of how we ran around

Chasing monsters in our underwear!

I guess growing up is what we do,

But if you happen to meet little Limbu & Timbu,

Tell them I'll be waiting near

The swing under the Mango tree.

# Learning to Fly

There is so much to write on, so much to do,

But still, I lay here not wanting to move,

My mind keeps poking saying

why are you wasting so much time and

My head says only just a little more while...

Those are quite frustrating moments if you know

What I am talking about and life goes on...

But when you do think of all the time you

Haven't been strong enough to just do what you

Are supposed to do, you feel you don't have a purpose

And how could you have just laid back

And watch the world pass by...

It's not about what you do,

It's not about what you have,

Neither is it about what others want you to have...

Your search for happiness or contentment is the
same as

A bird trying to find the sky, which is right around its
life...

So, it's not about seeing or knowing your way,

But learning how to fly,

Learning to be positive to lighten up your spirit

So you can fly your own way...

# A Daydream

Watch the clouds just passing by,

How they drift not wondering why,

You don't need a reason,

Just let go, try and fly...

Telling you what to do,

You can't just drift along

For you will be lost...

So what? There is no one watching your back.

# Chocolates

A poem for you...

For the way, you made me feel today...

A friend by my side I had,

Knew from his touch

How much he cared today...

Sweet nothings I tried

To whisper from my silence...

To tell you that I think

Of you, time and again...

These special trophies

Aren't just savings for a rainy day,

They are as they say,

Life's box of chocolates,

And you never know which

Flavour you might get one day...

But I enjoyed the one today...

# The Lover

"I see you turn away and I can't stand it, I would do anything to have your eyes on me again, even if it means destroying my heart, mind, body and soul.

Truly, madly, profoundly, that's all that I have ever known, to love and be loved is all that I need to survive in this world, tormented by hands that are so willing to let go.

Passions run high when gratitude is deep; devotion churned when love has faith's blessings."

# The Beauty Of A Soul

By the soul, we should trust our

Friends and know, beauty within

Can last forever. It is a soul

That can recognize another and make you

Feel in peace forever.

Why be so true for the things unknown,

For we have no knowledge of who is

Right or wrong;

You can only try to start something new

And discover for yourself what makes you

So sure, that the soul you have chosen

Is for you so true.

There are so many paths that you can

Explore but all of them will not

Make you so sure, and then you must know that

There are still places to go,

Or you can just fight through them all

And see for yourself the soul that you are.

# Losing

After all the things I have lost...

Of all the things I have let go...

You alone have been the

Sweetest thing...

The elixir that keeps me going...

The reflection of the lights

On the floor...

My muse, when all is vain...

My pride when all is strained...

In you, I shall always reside...

A part of me that will smile...

Even when I am losing...

Losing myself to you...

# A Promise

I love you, for I may say,

"Oh darling you have me, I wish for

What I seek, and it is you.

You are the moon of my nightfall,

You are the star of loving my all,

You are the ocean in my heart;

My love, I shall give you my love,

For the night is too short and the day too long.

For you shall be my pride one day,

For you shall be my friend today

And you shall be my love every day.

This is what I must ask you of

To unite together forever so far,

To make that day forever, it may be.

For I shall be your moon and you the sky,

Forever shall I be your loving and all."

I give this day my promise to you,

I shall be in love forever with you.

# Till Death do me Apart

Fear knocking on my door yet again

As I inch closer to you as I lay awake

The thought of parting away

Brings tears flowing down my way

First, I try to keep away, so that

My sobs don't bring you awake

But can't seem to keep my hands away

So, I put my arm around your chest

And bury my head into your neck

Your warmth makes me realize

What I will miss in those lonely nights

While you lay here and I there

Who will then I make conversations with

And who will put my mind at rest...

I can't seem to find a way

To reduce my anxious thoughts

Can't seem to sleep knowing that

I won't be able to cook you some lunch...

So long I had waited for you to come true

I have never loved anyone so truly

As I love you...

Would you always know this?

Would you know that you are everything

That I hold dear...

For you, I shall build a better world,

For you, I shall be there no matter what the

World will say...

So many stories I want to build with you,

So many dreams have to yet come true,

Would you wait for me as I have in return?

Do you know how difficult this is for me?

I can't seem to find enough words...

I just hope you know I love you,

Like no one else has loved for I know I will

Always belong to you...

Against all the odds I have fought to be with you,

And yet again I shall smile and find ways to

Be with the one who has been my kind...

You're the one who knows me inside out,

You're the one who I love exploring from dusk to dawn...

I see our unborn children every time you smile,

I see our dreams come true whenever I close my eyes...

I seem to distrust all of god's plans which

Pull me away from you,

But then I tell myself, it's through him that I met you...

So I keep my faith and hold on tight, knowing

No matter where I am, there is one thing that fear can't touch...

The love I feel for you will never diminish,

You are my song and my music,

You are the air that I breathe, it's your thought

That keeps me sane when things go wild...

I love you deeply as the snowflake is to the snow...

Without you, I am the Kero heater without the flame...

Silly I maybe, filled with flaws I maybe,

But I have loved you with all my heart,

That much I am sure of in this uncertain world,

That I shall love you till death do me apart...

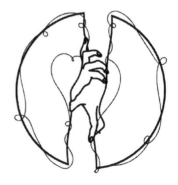

# Jhelum...

Why is that your waters taste so sweet...

The sound of your rushing,

Matches the beats of urgency,

The memories that you hold,

Bare witness of stories untold,

Would you keep him safe?

Watch over him as he washes his face...

Let no evil befall him,

Be the lullaby of my voice,

As he sleeps under the night sky,

Oh Jhelum, I wish I could

Flow as agile & swift as you,

Then maybe I could reach my

Beloved and drain the waters

That brings salt to my lips...

You're the only one who knows,

The depths of our hearts,

Show us again how you

Meander through the valleys

Of life, and have faith that

Every river has a shore...

# Longing

There is no one in my life yet,

Not that special someone yet,

No one who I can hug and cherish,

No one to call mine nor to belong in someone's heart yet,

But when I hear a song that touches that lonely girl in me,

Or see a heartfelt scene in other's stories...

How beautiful and complete life can be when

Someone would love a silly girl like me,

What an adventure it would be to have someone

To share and create new memories and experiences with,

Dew just seems to appear in my eyes longing

For that special someone to come and

Wipe it away to make it into a diamond ring...

# Hoping No More

Every time the phone rings,

Every time the doorbell rings,

I am waiting for you

I am waiting for you.

Every time I hear a knock

Or hear someone call,

I am hoping it's you

I am hoping it's you,

But to my grief

You never turn up,

You never do care.

I am tired of waiting for you,

I am tired of hoping it's you

To be the one from my dreams,

To be the one for whom I care

And to come to me when always

You know I am there.

# Caress my Soul

Here now, don't fear now

Caress my soul somehow,

Let go, don't let go,

Let the wings take us ashore

Faith now, have faith now , Nothing can tear us down

See now, see me now, I just want to be found

Silver shining dusky moon,  Heavens under perilous doom...

You've given all your might,

Nothing is left but a crescent Hope.

Innocent tears to undo the past

You'll be there when I close my eyes,

Yet again my heart calls to you,

Give me the strength to sail through the ruse...

Silver shining dusky moon, Heavens under perilous doom...

You've given all your might,

Nothing is left but a crescent Hope

Free from the condescending acts,

I'll never fit in the magician's hat.

Running wild I dive in the sky,

Nothing more to hold me back.

Wishing upon a shooting star,

All of what I could've changed so far,

Lying beside you, no frown to be found,

Here now, don't fear now,

Caress my soul somehow...

Let go, don't let go,

Let the wings take us ashore.

Faith now, have faith now

Nothing can tear us down...

# Trying Not To Try

I try so hard to please everyone,

I try so hard to make them like me

But I see that no one is there for me.

Why should I care to like anyone?

HE too has hexed me, not letting

Anyone love nor be loved by me.

But I still feel I should not do wrong;

What if someone feels bad? What if

Someone feels I am

Wrong.

I can't stand to try so very hard.

If I am mean, but not on purpose,

Will it still be my fault?

What if then by choice I Jinx,

Will I be going not to heaven?

How should I be,

I do not know, For I have lost myself in

Trying so many things.

But everything is going my opposite

Way and now I know not what more to say.

# Loops

You can check out when you want,

But you can never leave,

The beats of a familiar sound,

The brush of lead against the paper,

Somewhere it brings peace...

These little things we once knew,

In closed spaces, they show you,

That crack from the blue door,

Where light seems to peep at you,

In this game of hide and seek we play with ourselves,

Forgetting as we run around in circles,

That the room we created for "me",

The efficacy of privacy seems to be our own rivalry...

For one who does care of all that there is,

Shouldn't be doing so if he really did care,

For as they say true love is the one that is never shown,

You never have to leave the place you call home,

Because those circles you are running in,

It's just good practice for things to come....

We give reasons to make it alright

Or maybe write poems to make us feel real...

# Greener Someday

It's fear it's a heart-wrenching fear,

Ripping my soul apart,

That no one can love me the way you can,

Things would have been so much easier

If you were by my side, I wouldn't have

Had to struggle to make ends meet,

Would have had someone to talk to,

Even in the middle of the night...

But the complexity can't be undone,

I have lived through it, and you haven't,

So uninhibited I tell you to split your soul,

But at times like these,

All I want to do is run from home...

I fight, I beg him to love me,

But he seems lost in his own world,

Too distant from me,

I feel like a toy that he needs,

It's on his convenience that he chooses to love me...

It's then that I realize what I have missed,

It's then I know that never again, can I

Feel the magic on my lips and soul...

Never again can I be with you,

Though my heart aches to let you go...

I never planned for this,

But I will endure till the day I can,

And one fine day it will be the end of it all...

I know I can be happy,

It's just this excruciating phase

Of the grass being greener on the other side...

So, I breathe in, close my eyes,

And find you holding me and whispering

That it's going to be alright...

I just wish that you just knew,

That's how much I miss you...

I stare into someone else's eyes

And it wrenches my soul to see

You, in the eyes where there is no love to find...

So, I give you gallons of advice,

Keep your secrets, don't mention it to

Your side... for then you will be left

With broken dreams,

No one to love your truth, no matter how hard

You tried...

# A Thought

If I had any last words to say to you,

In this moment for the

First time they evade me.

Maybe because I have said everything

I have had to say...

And there are no regrets...

All I can say is...

I had a thought...

And it was about You...


*These are In Hindi. For my love for Urdu is evident even in tattoos.*


Itni bhi nafrat humse na karo...

Aap dusri duniya mein rehkar bhi

Humse hi shikayat karte ho...

Roothna aur manana hum bhi janate hai,

Aisa mat sochiye ki zindagi sirf

Aap ko hi nazar andaj karti hai...

Thokar toh sabhi insaan khate hai,

Jasba hum Rakhte hai, aasu peeke bhi,

Doosro ko hasane mein...

Dukh toh kambakht har koi deta hai...

Kabhi apne giribaan mein bhi dekhna,

Aise na ho, kisi ka gussa, aap kisi aur Pe,

Nikal dalo...

Itni, tez nighaho se aap Hume dekhte ho,

Pyaar nahi, berukhi abhi jhalakne lagi hai...

Hum koshish toh hazaar bar karte hai,

Par kya Kare, aap ko humara pyaar,

Humesha jhoota hi lagta hai...

Kabhi humse sachhi mohobat,

Karke toh dekhiye...Darr ke paar,

Aa ke toh dekhiye...

Shayad, fir aap samajh payenge...

Dil hatheli Pe hamesha humne,

Apna rakhha, aap fir bhi,

Hume hi Bolenge ki,

Ismein konsi nayi baat hai,

Aisa karna toh humari, Fitrat mein hai...

Yahan aap khamoshi ki panha lenge,

Aur hum kambakhat,

Dhoop ki dariyan mein bikhre hue milenge,

Dil aapka tab bhi na hum pighla payenge...

Chodiye, Dil todna koi aap se hi sikhe...

Intizar hi toh sirf hum kar sakte hai,

Ki shayad kabhi din, aap Hume

Samajh sake...

Kayamat bhi tabhi gawah hogi...

Kisi se bhi puch lijiye...

Itni mohobat humne, aap ke siva,

Kisi aur se kabhi na ki...


Sar bhi jhukaya, tane bhi Hazaron sune,

Aasu bhi bahaye, apna guroor bhi khud pi liya...

Sab kuch toh aap ko de baithe...

Isi aas mein, ki Shayad... Ek din, aap hume,

Vahi darja de, utna hi pyaar kare...

Jitna hum aapse karte hai...

# The Pole Star

Why do you always talk about going away...

Instead of saying let me pull

You closer and ease your pain...

Don't you see it's for you that I do the things I do...

No matter somehow things

Just spill

Without any clue...

But so quickly it seems you want

To disappear, and start life anew...

You think I don't fear that

All these miles you put between us...

Will eventually make you forget that I exist...

And when you do have what it is that you wish for,

In the corridors of beauty,

You'll see me fade into distant memory...

Do what needs to be done,

I'll never stop you even if you

Ask me to let go of your hand...

For by now, you should know

What lays behind the curtains...

Even if my dialogues don't match my intentions...

Say that it's ok to want you and I'll be

The Pole star which you will miss

On cloudy days...

And no matter in which direction,

You'll Still find the light to

Brighten up the horizon...

# No More

Can't come back now,

Can't say that I am yours...

So much of me you have lost,

You don't know how I was for so long...

I can't feel that feeling anymore.

I know you don't say your mine anymore...

My life will have new pages,

The one you wrote in will be the one,

In which the other half will always remain with you...

You can't hear what my heart tries to tell you secretly,

You will not know how I feel anymore,

The time has gone for me to say anything anymore...

# Buddy

It's a wonder how the things I love
Slip away from my hands,
No matter how tightly or loosely I
Hold the sand...
Each grain just seems to wither away,
And turn into dust...
You used to excite me, give me a rush
That would make me feel alive...
But all I feel now is a little dead inside...
For time seems to have halted itself for me...
But don't you worry, I have weathered
Many storms and this too shall pass...
At Least now am at peace that,
I finally have a buddy who I can
Talk to without all the negativity

Have come a long way,

To have the above dialogues between us...

I am glad and proud that we made it so far.

# By Your Side

Wherever you go, whatever you do,

Whatever you say I'll be by your side,

But I won't be there if you let me go.

Walking beside you holding your hand,

I'll be there for you if you give me your hand.

Telling you softly, I will be there for you.

Whatever you have done I'll be by your side only

If you let me be a part of your truth.

See how the stars make our dreams come true;

So far away, they let us be a part of their moon.

Lying beside you caring for you

I will show you our dream

If you want to walk beside me.

# Surrender

My heart I gave to you when you

Asked for it, knowing you would treasure it

As if it were your own

Your soul I knew was different from all and you

Taught me so many things

You too did say, you were different from all

And that is why you would never break my heart

I did try ever so hard to make us happy,

You were the first one who I would think of

First thing in the morning and that at night

Surrendered myself to you thinking

That would make you happy and in return

You would give me my happiness, and that is your
love...

I lost myself in you but instead of finding

Me I was pushed even deeper

Trying to change me into someone who I would
never be

All I asked was your love, love which you

Said you had for me; I know you did

But I don't understand why you would change
something

That would make me so happy!

I wanted love, which would bring me at peace

That is why I surrendered to you, my heart...

I am not weak; I am not afraid, and this is not

Why I fell in love with you, I surrendered all my love
to you

Now I shall not weep for the unfought battle that

I have lost and neither will I ever try to win it

I will set myself-free because love is not

A battle and never will it be for me

It will be the key to freedom for which I shall live...

# Sweet Dreams

Night has come, so I shall dream...

Without you being beside me...

No matter how things seem...

But in my dreams, my wishes may be seen...

# III

# PROVIDING ORDER

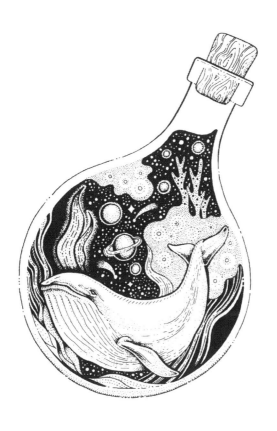

# The Altruist

"I see your tears and can't wait to hold you near,

Fiercely ill protect, even if you use me as you please,

For selfishness I abhor, ingratitude I loathe,

Very little, I need to survive. I can withstand the aridest
of desserts,

My heart is what ill put on a platter & care for you as
I turn to ashes."

# The Cuddle

These moments of wonder

That struck me half-past two,

Make me fuzzy

With a smile and words in my hand...

As I feel you gliding

In the space between my heart and core,

A thin layer of skin separating

My fingers from your little toes and wriggles,

I wonder what you would think of me,

When you see me...

Will you know how to love me?

I sure am learning all I can,

To love you with all the joy you deserve,

A little life that has yet to see the world,

Sent my way, with a purpose and a mystery,

I guess I'll not know until my dying is known...

A sweetness that flows, as I know,

Your hearing my heartbeats,

You seem to know everything that is going on

Inside of me...

You've made me fierce you've made me stronger,

Taught me to care for myself,

And I wonder why people say that we are the

Ones who teach the new founders...

It just seems to me I don't fit into

This world's scheme of things...

You've got to be smarter than me,

That's how Darwin said the world ought to work.

Rumi said you will rekindle the soul,

Tony said the energies must flow,

Papa believes in happiness of the whole,

Roscoe barks for bones to grind,

The lotus blooms, reminding Mamma of her roots...

Will you be a he, will you be a she,

My mind says one thing and

My tongue gives way to Freudian slips...

Will, you have hair like the waves of papas lateral
thinking,

Will you have skin like mama's sense of fair justice...

The biblical stories and the legends of the Gita,

Both will be your roots,

I hope you take in the essence of what and what not to do...

No matter how hard I try to shield you,

I can't make promises cause life is

Something way bigger than me...

All I can say is, I'll try to teach you all that I can,

But mistakes are made, we are only human,

All we can do is take it in our stride and

Make lemonade with the lemons you got...

A lemon tree was never thought to be a good investment,

Now use all your imagination to convert it

Into a forest of ice cream

And all that you may learn to love...

And there will be times you'll get

A toothache with all the sweetness,

That time it's ok to rub your eyes when

The spice brings you close to tears...

There always will be two sides to a coin,

A silver lining no matter how entangled the vine...

It would be ok to escape and fly into an adventure,

It would be ok to freeze and lose a few moments,

It would also be ok if you find yourself in a fight,

Fret not if no one's on your side,

Just make sure you win cause

History is written in the shape

Of the skills that you would be using...

If you lose, know that 70 per cent is water, intangible,

And life is made of crests and troughs

That you ride on with your heart, mind and soul...

When in doubt just choose and accept the consequences,

Trust yourself because I will always believe in you...

When the advice gets too much, just turn out the noise,

Put on the music that you like and

Make a melody that would fit perfectly

To the lyrics, you want to sing...

I will always be there no matter what,

No force in this world can change that

You are the child that I have always loved ...

I saw you in my future, I see you in my past,

I feel you in my present,

Just waiting to meet you now so

That we can make some magic together

That will be a metaphor for all that we experience ...

The potential to change the course of our lives,

Take a turn and find a new story

That will enliven us to spread it to the moon and the stars...

While the sun gently shines brightly on us...

And papa bear cuddles us with his unconditional love...

# The Midnight Prose

It's 10 pm two hours from where this year comes to an
end ...

The blower is on,

A hope that the coming year will be filled with

Warm encounters that will lift up the heart ...

My baby is awfully sleepy,

Making sounds that bring urgency to

The deeds that need to be fulfilled...

But I continue to write cause words are my only solace

As I smile at his face, so he knows he will always have
me...

But far away once where Mercury walked the beaches,

Half part of my soul lingers around over the Azure
waters,

My eyes on the love that made so many things
possible ...

The twinkling string of lights over the dinner table
seem so inviting...

Finally, the echoes of the DJ and

Music playing seems to drown down, with my writing...

The thought of people getting together while

I stay surrounded by the tokens I have collected to decorate

What I call now a home, Seems rather distressing,

The Merry spirit now envying on how others can go on

While I am still picking up the pieces...

The fun things I have missed while

I was too busy thinking of contingencies...

But the glow in the dark stickers,

Which are about to become visible,

Usher the Midnight sleep...

I'll be dreaming while the world would be screaming.

Now that doesn't seem such a bad thought at all...

Only if the mind is kind enough to give me sweet memories...

# The Little Moongusie

My feet are up, after a long day,

You are dreaming just right beside me,

The cradle with a cloud of net,

It's winter, so you have your head

Covered in a jacket made of day...

I wonder how old you'll be,

I hope these words do reach you

Wherever you may be...

In this uncertain world, I don't know,

If I will be around,

But one thing I know for sure you will always be my Sun...

Can't find the words to let you know,

How you gave me a purpose when everything

Crumbled down to dust...

Don't want to walk past the memory lanes,

But I still feel I need you to know that the world is not
as it seems ...

You'll discover love in the most unlikely places,

And you'll find horrors right under your nose...

So, Walk as I have taught you to walk...

Your head held high but your feet knowing your ground...

It will be my endeavour to show you all the ways of this world,

Make you survive so that you find your own purpose...

However, don't try too hard to keep looking for it,

No one really has a clue as to what we should really do...

But one thing I know... This moment I want to freeze...

A snowflake that would capture,

The beginning of your childhood...

I feel blessed to be a mother,

Everyone finds their child to be spectacular...

But it's not just words, I have proof,

My child is like no other...

I have known this since you were in my tummy,

Could feel a sense of energy,

Like the sun shining on me...

I felt no pain, it was as if you were disguised, and

No one could see the little magician in my veins...

At 3 months, you look at me as you drink your meals,

Your eyes saying so much,

I fail to decode everything you feel...

Never a whale, but little cries,

Letting me know,

That you aren't fussing about just to gain attention,

Quietly you learn to sleep by yourself,

In your rocking chair ...

Your laughter is the shrills that

Would heal and scare the most wicked of dreams,

Telling them, you're not someone who is to be messed with ...

The smiles you give me when you see me around,

I can make it out in your eyes that

You want to be held and taken around...

You've got mine and your Papas curiosity,

That's been something that

Has been a trait since you have been breathing...

The entire world you would capture if given a chance,

I have a feeling you will become a great explorer...

You would put even an adult to shame,

That's how aware you are of

What goes around in your den...

The slightest of movements, light and sound...

Nothing escapes your charismatic waves...

I often wonder if that's how babies are supposed to be,

But to me, you seem like an old soul

That has been sent to do something meaningful in this world...

But I tell myself, not to burden you with silly expectations,

Cause my life went being a slave

To others insidious altercations...

But I have no regrets anymore,

Cause you gave me the courage to rise from the ashes...

Didn't really believe that

Babies could have such potential...

But now I know why they say

God resides in these miraculous anatomies.

You are taking your time to reach out

To the things that fascinate you,

But go all in once you hear the music

Of the relaxed ambience...

You take time to get to know people,

But once you do,

You'll smile and then shy away knowing not what to do...

I often wonder if you will change or stay the same...

No matter what you say or do

I will love you just the same...

When it's time to rest you may

Not necessarily go into the night softly,

Your dreams are a quick reflection

On how your day has been...

You have the voice of a night angel,

Experimenting with it as you do with your Riyas...

Followed by some real energetic flying,

Yes, when I see you move like that

It seems you're almost flying in thin air...

You have your little friends tiggy owly and birdy,

You talk to them,

In the hope that they respond in the same frequency...

You do your hummm with your chin turning up,

As if asking me,

Mum, why don't you pick me up and let's do something exciting ...

You are my adventure,

One who is inspiring to give wings to my venture...

I love the identity you have given me,

A mother, I hope I can really be...

Don't have any role models to raise you by,

But I know that you will turn out just fine...

Cause it's me who is telling you,

And trust me I have been enough
in this world

To know what I am saying...

# Mother's Day

Within the heart of a mountain there

Is it a fountain of precious stones?

Within the heart of the earth, there is

The mirth of gold;

Within the heart of the sky, there are

Flying diamonds;

But within my heart, there is your love

Fortified with the blood in my heart.

Your care, love, tenderness will be evermore.

What mothers love can do has been seen till ever now,

The kindness in her eyes,

The concern in her hands,

The tenderness in her kiss has

Blessed my heart.

On an auspicious day like this a poem, I write to you

Thanking you for everything you have done for me,

For asking for forgiveness for the wrong things

I have done till now,

And to tell you, you are the best mom in the world.

# The Doctor

I am small and little, but my heart calls out loud,

About a young river who knew not its path then,

Just flowed over where the land called,

It did hold dreams of abundant land,

But storms and barren land is what it got,

It thought of shattered dreams...

But did it not realize that each storm it conquered

Each desert it passed by, it made it stronger

And created an oasis, a dream fulfilled

Not of its mind but a different kind,

Created with unconditional love,

Spreading joy in the lives of the people it touched and transformed...

Maybe not a thousand as it expected but at least mine...

Perhaps you couldn't help a million people in need

But you made the most beautiful home in the world

For the children who needed you the most...

The love, care, mistakes you forgave and forgot of others,

The sacrifices, troubles that you bore are far much more

You could give to the people around you by being the

Most wonderful person you are, who is independent

Confident original in her beliefs, thoughts and work,

And the most amazing and hardworking homemaker

I respect and love the most...

Destiny brought you a different way to complete a picture

Of the perfect mom, who has always practised

And given the right treatment when one was sad,

Has the ideal prevention plan to not let us fall,

Who gives the correct advice to heal mind and soul...

All in all, the perfect and best-learned doctor and practitioner

I have known...

# My Little Elf

With his little walk, with his little talk

He wins my heart with his little laugh.

His eyes look like precious black pearls

His lips look like pink rose petals

His little hands, his little feet

What he does with his not so tiny plea

Is something of a wonder

Which he crawls along on,

Wanting to hold everything he can feel

Wanting to eat everything he sees,

Little tantrums that he throws

Are like little red flower he blows

His crying can make the world go round

Or make it drown with a tender soul.

Softer than velvet his skin is

Innocent as an angle he is.

# Bruvver

For years I was alone,

But 15 years back this day,

I was gifted with an angel with

The heart of gold

And the mischief of a devil,

Was lucky to see you grow up,

From the child, you were to the

Boy, now you have become.

Proud to see the strength you have shown,

When you stood up against all the odds.

I wish you all the happiness that could be,

The protection of a blessing to help you,

Sail through the storms.

This day was when I was blessed with

My twin soul, the same flesh and
blood

That I would call my Bro :)

# A Special Bond

There are those who can reach out to millions;

They have

Fairy dust that makes others

enchanted by them,

There is a bond between a star and the admirer,

Which is so unique that whenever the

Star reaches out, it makes an admirer like me so
complete within.

All of my

Worries, all of the sadness

All of the desperation just

Disappeared somehow, and a feeling

Of wonderment, has been filled in my heart.

A complete stranger

Who managed to capture my heart;

A sweet memory to be cherished.

Waiting to meet someday,

But it does not matter even if that is eluded.

I can still be a part of what they are,

Through the wonders that they spread.

# I Wish

Through the tides of time,

The waves of life...

You have surfed and raised above.

The crests and troughs...

The reluctant artist

And the practical philosopher.

You've filled Rhythm into my life

To which I can dance away my blues

It's not every day that I get

Humbled in gratitude

To celebrate a moment in

The Space & Time Quantum

Where I wish

May all your pending wishes come true.

# I Love You

From the moment I have known you,

You have brought love into my life

And no one can love me in the way which you have,

for you can only be loved and only more,

You are my soul, you are my conscience

You are my life.

You turned my tears into stars,

You fulfilled my pleading wishes,

You gave me strength, you gave me hope,

You gave me your faith; you gave me your self

And it only hurts me more to know if

I have hurt you, for which I may give a kiss and say
sorry, But I have loved you from the core of my heart,
and it's only your touch; it's only your
love That I wish for,

For which I may give my heart and say

I love you, and now there is nothing that
I want more.

# Falling

In your eyes, I can see my world complete,

In your arms, I feel my dreams being fulfilled,

What words should I tell my darling,

Who already knows the way I feel...

But just because he already knows,

Doesn't mean I can't tell him how much,

Am still in love with him...

Every day I imagine you by my side,

The revolutions this earth takes,

Isn't what completes my twenty four hours,

It's your thoughts, it's your call,

That you make to me, that lets me know,

That my day has passed...

Like a little girl, I tell you all my secrets,

In the treasure box of your heart, I know,

They will remain all hidden...

It's a wonder how you keep all my secrets hidden,

That is how I know my treasure box is fathomless within;

Your heart is like an ocean...

The permission you have given me to swim within,

Let's me explore a whole new vision,

You do not know how blessed I feel with,

The love you shower upon me...

My life you give me with those kind words that you speak,

How do I resist this charm,

With which you still mesmerize me,

I really can't help falling in love with thee...

# Season of Winter

Season of winter thou comest now

With chaos and freeze,

With unworthy treasures

Of sadness and moan.

Thou aren't aware of the hurt.

That has been brought,

From the land unknown.

Season of winter has brought pain,

Thee can't imagine but

My trust for my love will never fade,

I will forever stand beside my beloved

For seasons to come.

# The Second Sun

The memories shared,

Are but like the

Stories weaved of the

Constellations great...

The ever afters with ironies

That makes up for the

Legendary epiphanies,

Like the forgotten shores

Of the untamed Rivers,

But a reminder that

Sweet symphonies can be made

Of lost treasures...

The travels in time machines

Of daydreams, a hint to

Calm the storms when they

Thunder louder than rationality...

Sweet reminders that, smiles

Shall prevail even in the oddest

Of pickles, for grace is the

Dawn of humility, by which

We have made it so far to

Still see the rise of a second Sun...

# A Story of you and Me

My mind is in turmoil, I can feel the not so distant
pain,

Can't take it anymore, my wits split in half...

The fear of choosing the wrong path,

A mistake I wouldn't be able to undo...

The pain & hurt in my heart can't

Be shared by the innocent mist...

Never had I planned to hurt anyone,

Never wanted to be in such a helpless state...

Alone I felt, no one to share my burden;

No human touch to comfort;

No one to understand the pain;

No one to help resolve my battling mind...

I have been in pain before...

Feel so scared thinking, that

Happiness could have been a mere illusion...

I have seen in this world where

A hand never reaches out to help a soul,

Cruelty does last, and death seems more natural to
have had...

So how can a simple me expect to be happy again,

Knowing that there is no place

Even for a tender heart in this world

Drowned in cruel games...

But a kind voice I can sense through all this wreck,

My Lord is now speaking to me

Through his coincidental ways...

He brings calm to my threatened heart,

I can see the courage rising

As I hold on to the silver thread...

I can hear myself speak of forgiveness,

I can feel the urge to stand back up again,

for it is not rational to think that

There are no more paths to walk on,

When you're still walking on land!

I can see him smiling at me,

He seems to be happy that

I didn't misunderstand him,

I feel at peace when I realize that

It was through the pain that

I have come to see his miracles of love,

Courage & dreams coming true...

He shares with me his mysterious ways,

From which I know it's not that he is playing,

Instead, it's only cause and effect...

Some things are meant to happen,

It's nothing personal... But still, he favours me...

I think it's because I have learnt to see

the pure-hearted sky

Behind the purpose-filled clouds...

I Believe he Does...

That is why he Does favour me.

# The Ruler

"I see your chaos and can't wait to set some method to the madness,

I will fiercely accept if am challenged to a duel. Heed to me, and all will be well; power needs to exude if the rivers of prosperity are to be untethered.

Don't question me; it's got to be done my way; power isn't everything; it's the Only thing that matters to surmount the throne."

# The Lost Love

Every choice you make is away from me,

Unwittingly or knowingly no matter

How hard you try; love doesn't come easy.

There seems to be a pleasure that satiates you,

When you find yourself denying me things...

A sense of power and security when you know,

I long for love, respect and affection...

If I say a word, it's met with silence,

It's greeted with a deaf ear and a glance that

Would never see the light of day...

Busy somewhere else, fighting in the unreal world,

Or distancing itself from the stuffed atmosphere,

The ambience never seems to be right when I come into the room...

You ask me what's wrong, I nod my head with a heavy heart...

What do I say to the man who promised me love,

Companionship and happiness...

But now I am left, an inconvenient truth that makes him feel

Restless as he is split between his morality and responsibility...

The free spirit in him seems to be shackled by me,

He lets me know this quite often...

A trifling burden, a dark cloud as if hanging around his neck...

He seems to feel helpless at the predicaments I face...

What do I do, when the knight in the shining armour,

Turns around and says I need to walk along with everyone,

Being just by your side is not who I am...

So, I pick myself up, every night out of my bed...

I see him resting and tired because he has been stressed...

I silently pick up my crying child,

Wondering what I would say to him if I were to narrate to him,

The pain and loneliness I have been gifted with...

Choices that I have to live with of the things his fate decides ...

However, every choice I make, it always has to prove a point...

Standing as if in the court box,

Providing evidence of my undying love...

Longing for that hug, the genuine care that should come naturally ...

But somehow, it's got lost, and the sand is now in my eyes.

Turning me into the person who seems needy,

Making me the scapegoat when they don't want to take responsibility,

Questioning my motives when they lose foresight,

Turning the table on me when they can't fulfil the expectations,

Calling me irrational when their inner child throws a tantrum...

Loving me only when it is convenient...

And I do things as per their liking...

May it be a strand of short hair, may it be a serial that I cherish,

May it be finding a home for myself,

Or wanting a soldier by my side...

All I receive are the comments with flying arrows,

None of them ever seeking to penetrate the truth that I am.

Just superficial care that lacks depth,

A heart that can't show empathy but expects that I show unconditional loyalty...

But I wonder where the loyalty lies when priority is never me...

And this question will be met by saying...

You will never understand me...

And then I think to myself,

Yes, I will never understand a heart that never opened up to me.

A love slowly losing its touch...

Sparks now replacing cold embers,

Memories that seem to be tainted by selfish acts.

Choices that were made for me,

Under the pretext of what was best for me,

But the hidden self-righteousness took away even my dignity...

One good deed you do,

You want me to remember it over the fifteen stabs you give to my heart...

Fifteen good deeds I do,

You remember only the one where you felt I hurt your pride.

# The Crater Half of the Moon

I looked at the sun today
Behind the veil of clouds,
Found it pale as compared
To a moonlit night,
As the raindrops still soothe
The surface below the heavens,
A cool breeze reminds me
Of the once torched bosoms,
I feel like a woman scorned
Even with his slightest blink,
His eyes I want on me
Of every day and minute,
If not, I reign down fury
With a shower of tears,
Even though not at fault
He fulfils all my wishes…
A man's kindness I never knew
Could melt a storm,

Never knew that a man could nurture

A wild child with faith such divine,

All sins would drown...

Makes me wonder, think of all my wrongs,

How on earth did I deserve

Such blessings from tender hands...

These words I write to let him know,

Never have I been so loved

Or loved so much....

The tantrums I throw are subdued

By your forgiveness,

The fights I build are cushioned

With your wit,

The pain is healed with your kind words,

The restlessness calmed

With the faith, you show in us...

I know I can't demand patience all the time,

Nor sorries can take away the hurt

Caused by sharp-edged words each time...

But I am willing to shed away all my flesh and bones,

To hold your hand and build you a home,

Each day I will stand by you,

Wait for you in the heavens if it is,

Take away all the burden that there is,

So that I can be,

The crater that completes the moon...

# The Frenemy

There are those fair-weather friends,

Which put you in doubt...

"Am just telling you the truth you know,

Frankness is what I believe & cherish."

And then you wonder about your insufficiency,

While they gloat on burdens, they have been under,

Then the light bulb ignites to make you realize,

They were busy manipulating you,

To get precisely what serves their scheming minds...

Never can they see the goodness in the world,

For they victimize themselves of

The harshness that they were brought under,

Justifying that's the reason

They are so 'practical' in their ways,

And that's why it's not a big deal if

They are rude in their days...

Cribbing Is their passion and

Stonewalling is their ultimate deception,

However, if they are in a mood to criticize and cry,

You're expected to hear it all with all the right sighs...

God forbid if you say no to them,

Their ego is bruised with a thousand pens,

Then they will make sure to teach you a lesson,

For giving back two folds is their war motivation...

The hypocrisy is at its heights when

You need them, and they say,

Your over-sensitive and naive, for they seem to
have seen

Yhe world and know something about everything.

When there is some favour, they would like to ask,

You wonder how the hyena has turned into

The Vodafone pug,

Which won't rest until the work has been done...

But should you ever need a helping hand,

All you will get are unanswered and

'I am a little busy with something important' sort of
plans...

The best you can do is cut them loose,

For their self-esteem and insecurity cannot be healed

No matter how many minefields you walk through...

So, it's best you walk away, and tell them,

Meet you some other day,

For I have better things to do.

# Truth or Dare

I keep talking to myself,

As if you were listening...

Hallucinating your gaze,

All protective over me...

Feel like ten, on a swing,

With my best friend ...

But now all grown up,

I want to play behind closed doors...

Would you choose truth or dare?

What prize do we keep,

If you lose to me...

If you win, I know you'll

Want the locked door's key,

Or Won't you? Dare me ...

Will only truth leave your lips,

Will you have the strength

To complete the dares?

So, tell me, my righteous boy,

Don't you miss me like the forbidden tree?

Don't you wish like tearing me apart,

When I make you lose your mind,

All you want would be to pin me to a wall,

Say you like it when I pretend you to be my man,

Even if I am wrong, you never really,

Want me to stop...

I dare you to say, you want me,

Dare you to kiss me once and still not want more...

Dare you to find a girl, who can drive you crazy,

Love you as long and the way I have desired you...

Hate me more than what you have already hated then
pulling me close when you're most angry...

Forget me and let me drown in the river,

Say I am not what you have ever wanted...

Dare you to satisfy your every fantasy,

Not let me leave night after night...

Say that you want me to stop...

Here's the key, you're free to go...

Know that this chase will never be complete...

Like the ghosts of time, I will surrender

Each time you call out to me,

Say that I don't want you until you

Blame me for all of your misery...

Tell me the things you think when you close your eyes,

Do you think I can't feel them,

Just because I'm away a thousand miles...

Each breath you take, every word you say,

Resonates in my universe, telling me

You need me right now to fulfil your desires,

It's never enough, the further away, the closer

We get... the closer we are, we forget the rest...

Before you accuse me of being a witch...

Tell me, did I ask you to read all this?

You came in search of me,

Your every wish is my destiny...

Tell me, won't you again read this?

This time, enjoying every bit...

The guilt is not enough to hold you at bay,

Let the restrain fall, or I dare you to

Cuff me to whatever is there,

Would you punish me if I don't obey,

If not, tell me why I can't have my way?

Urge me to make mistakes,

Urge me to sin, for I don't want to live

In a world where you don't belong...

All this is only a small glimpse to

Show you how much I need you...

In truth, I don't want any of it,

If you don't want...

This is the only way I can show my love,

But don't think it's only about lust...

It's only a fraction of everything I feel...

I can go without passion, but your soul

Is calling out to me...

Which language do I then speak to

Hear you out... to let you know,

You don't have to fear, I will never leave

Your side ...

But what will you do, when I grow unsure?

What will you do when I grow old?

It's not me, but you who has forgotten me...

To you, all I am is a Maggie point...

I have been cast aside like your worn out first Wife,

Never did you ever want me,

Then why do I still convince myself...

A fool is all that you think of me,

A girl with no restraint or control...

You can't even see me for who I am,

And here I am willing to give you everything I have...

So No, I don't want you if you don't want me,

These silly words will never reach your custody...

Dare me never to love you...

All you ever said was, you don't love me...

But I never said you did,

All I said was, you never said that I didn't ...

Think of it as a lie... think that I want to leave the room...

Think that I don't want your lips on mine,

Think that your ghost stopped visiting you forevermore...

Would that make you happy?

Or would me turning to face you with the door behind my back...

Without the key to find... Will make you sleep?

Do you know what words I need to rest my head on the pillow??

Forget it, it's better when I talk to myself...

Don't worry, I don't want anything from you anymore...

Even I can't keep walking on knives if you don't hold me back...

So, let's just laugh it off... and go back to being

Ten-year-olds...

# The Hurricane

As I stood there, with my palms against the wall,

My head lowered, the sprinkling water,

Soaking my hair...

I had a smile on my face, the devilish one,

Felt in sync with my soul, as my body was

Being caressed with pearls of water...

I was fascinated with the fact that

I still wanted you even when I had just

Helped myself to a fantasy where you

Spoke the words I needed to hear...

I wondered if it was the same with you...

Would you still cuddle me, even when

Your needs were met...

I didn't know the answer, though I know how it feels,

After we are done, you do give a hug but always in a rush...

But the silence you reward me with,

After the exchange of letters,

Makes me feel that you don't feel my

Need after you reach your threshold...

So, does it mean, I have always wanted you more?

Am I just a plaything or I mean much more...

That lets me think of all the questions and

Answers that go through a human's mind...

Another reason I give myself is,

You always did say that distance makes the

Heart grow fonder, you never liked me, you preferred the chase better...

Your sadistic need to deny yourself

What makes you happy,

But I still recollect when you did say,

Show me how much you feel for me...

But that too wasn't the question...

How did I work out the arithmetic...

Well in the absence,

I have more time for me to think...

A= c and b = c hence, a = b ...

Meaning, only if you love one can you love another,

If you despise one, you despise the other,

None better than the other...

A split personality of the same soul...

But yes, the distance makes it easier...

To forget, to relive, to pause while the time holds still...

My turn too will come, when I will need to share

You... but it won't be complicated,

Knowing myself, I would rather enjoy it...

I haven't seen anyone on your arm,

It will make me happy to see you hold another's hand...

A sense of relief that he isn't just my responsibility,

Relief! I don't have to provide for social,

Economic or culinary skills...

Don't look at me like that! Believe me when I say...

Never have you ever bought me a gift,

You enjoy the attention, without having to

Take me for dinners or give flowers and books...

You come in as you please, leave as you please,

No strings attached just the way you like it...

For me, I too have become used to it now,

Not depending on you for much,

That's why I can't leave what I have got,

I treasure it because I too have my promises to keep...

But yes, I do take a deep breath when you give a pause,

It is excruciating, but just like a needle when we need the shot...

Just like a long kiss and then you need a breath of fresh air...

Once I wake up from the daydream,

I have my work and responsibilities that ground me...

But the wait for the next sip of lemonade,

Makes me feel like a fool as well as thankful...

I wonder if we ever will be able to kiss,

Without the need of taking constant oxygen breaks...

Wonder if you do think about these things,

Or just compartmentalize and blame me

For the hurricane that hit the scene...

Yes yes, I do feel the guilt, I break up in tears and the smile...

But it's nice with the water over me...

I am not a child; I know how to swim...

So, hope you get what I am saying,

Now let me out, if you're done with the shower,

Need to dry myself afresh to lose your scent...

But the kiss on the forehead will stay where it is...

Need to get up, dress up and show up for dinner...

# The Giant

I have grown like a giant...

Lonesome and unsure...

The need to teach my self

Has got me through the

Citadels of Rome...

I still need more...

Someone to share my dreams,

Someone who can mind read,

Someone to call mine...

Until something is found wrong with me...

Nothing I do seems right,

My desires curbed out of sight...

I did all I could,

I ate until I wasn't starving...

I asked cupid,

If he could throw one at me,

But he pushed me away,

While he cast thirty-six arrows,

None of them meant for me...

Like a child, I pleaded,

But he didn't want anything

To do with me...

A crate full of desires, passions

Dreams and fantasies,

I am called the epitome

Of greed and vanity...

The one with Alice's allegory,

For others can't seem to match my theme...

So am running in circles,

Being told it's no one's business,

Finally, I shake my clavicle and blades

To spread my wings and take flight,

I fly enough to really have oversight...

No more a giant, am a Titan...

A Titan with wings of steel...

It's then I feel my core,

All I want to do is love even more...

Make my shoulders strong enough...

To carry the weight of others rocks...

Have you heard of rocks turning into feathers,

When rhythm brings a smile in your favour...

They go their way,

I go mine...

But do I hear footsteps,

Following behind...

I take the blame; I hear the sane...

But in the end,

I am the Titan that found the

Celestial Plane...

# The Artist

*"I see not just you, but all the versions of what you can become, I would craft destiny to bend it at my will, only if, excellence was envisioned even by mediocrity.*

*To see your creation come alive is like opium that blurs reality, it takes you across dimensions and eternity. A fierceness drives me to complete my masterpiece.*

*The earth will always remain the magnificent handy work of an artist, even in my tomb, I would crave an embrace of the one and only."*

# Pencil

I'll give you a pencil, tell me what you see

For one can read what others can't see

I see a sea in this pencil I hold,

Surrounding a mountain whose top

Is made of black snow, I am the

Creator, I can tilt the sea and the mountain,

To cover what I want with its dark core

With darkness to still give exuberant light

What I make it can always be undone, what I keep will

Be paths to new worlds,

Its end I can feel to make me think, on its

Journey I will hold to make it my friend,

It comes from the same earth from where I have been raised

My pencil is sturdy so I can use it. It will

Break but never bend. But sometimes I feel

It's wise to bend than break...

But there are the ways which a pencil has

And so many more, which I may not see...

It is what it is no other

Name can own it, but it will not change

From what it is...

# Ying & Yang

The strokes you make with your hand,

The led ever so softly brushing against

The canvas of life,

I eagerly waiting to see the colours you will fill in my life,

Coaxing the reluctant artist in you

To find a muse,

To lighten up the flame that glows

Within you

It keeps me warm day and night...

The silence that dances softly

When no words leave our lips,

I can see you from the corner of my eyes

Assured that your there right by my side,

A sense of happiness washes over me

A refreshing wave from the dreary world outside...

I never want you to leave our nest,

Never to lose the sight of you,

The smiles you bring,

Last for the longest time...

Lying beside me, Cuddled in your arms,

taking photographs to

Freeze these moments in time...

Not knowing what's to come ahead,

Looking back on how things have been,

Being right now and here with you,

As you work on your masterpiece,

A piece of your soul that I will always have with me...

Each stroke you make,

The pencil brushing against the white sheet,

Reminding me of the times, you caress me...

Every-time you pick up the eraser,

I am assured it's all going to turn out to be better,

The way we move past our mistakes unwavering of
whatever may be in our way,

The way you adjust your stance to get into position to
be able to draw the perfect orb,

Reminds me of the time we swallow our pride and
anger

To give each other the best of what we can,

Not wanting to hurt but protect our hearts and fill
them with the love we promised

As we kneeled at the altar...

As you start to fill the colour into the blank spaces,

Your fingers now have tightened their grip over the wooden elixir,

Every intention now stated with clarity,

A resolve to pave a path to all our dreams,

Undeterred to the distractions outside,

But still thoughtful enough to see if everything is alright...

This is the man that I have loved, this is the man I choose to love...

Ever so silently, unknowingly, he inspires me to be the best of what I can be...

And I love him for everything that he is...

I Try not disturbing him,

I want him to be himself in my company,

Nor do I encroach into the mechanics of his mind,

A mystery that I wish to discover through eternity...

And then I hear him blow away the specs of stardust,

The drawing almost complete,

I resist my urge to peek in,

Knowing that I want it to be a surprise when I marvel at his handy work,

A beautiful picture which he has drawn just for me...

I write along, making my piece lengthy,

So, I too have something worthwhile to give him,

To let him know, I had been thinking all along about him,

Cherishing each moment, savouring every breath that we share together...

Return all of his kindness which he deserves with every inch he covers...

He might say I play the balancing act,

But how do I tell him

That I want to love him as much as I can...

He seems to still have so much to give,

While my poem now seems to be complete...

All I want to do now is lean over him,

Watch him as he creates a life where we both live in.

Oh, what delight flows over me, my words seem to be resurrecting...

To see the colours he has filled,

I can't hold myself back from kissing his cheek...

At that, he says- wait am not done yet...

I watch in awe how a lamb can befriend a tiger ...

How the toughness envelopes the softest of desires...

Everything seems possible...

Even though I can hear the rain rustling outside...

He looks over at me with the innocence of a child,

I greet him with a big broad smile...

He goes back to his devout passion of the moment...

He then asks me - What do 'I' make of this,

Wanting to know what it is that I think...

I stumble upon my own words, not knowing what to say...

I gather my wits to say something...

Then realize I already had been working on the answer to what was on his mind...

That's how much in sync we are,

No matter the words or distance that is exchanged between us.

# The Sonnet

The hymns that I hear spread symmetry till my ears,

One day of rage followed by smooth sailing across the frays,

The enigma that still concocts wonder dust...

It enfeebles my already frazzled mind,

At the same time quaffs a thirst unmeasured by time...

The balls of crumpled paper,

Thrown away for they couldn't envisage my temper...

Now bear the seal of wax, guarding the chimerical

Sparks of cupid's darts...

Rhymes are lost in these irrevocable nights and days...

Words still seem fine to bring a smile to your face...

# World of My Own

Puzzle's, questions, mysteries, facts

The truth, lies, what and why,

Correct, wrong, complex, compound, yes or no;

I don't want to fall with so many words

Rotating my head with their revolving play.

Free and fast, I want to fly.

So, no one can catch me with all these nets.

What should I do, when I must do?

Why I should do how I must do,

I don't want to care.

This world I see with my

Own worthy eyes,

This world I feel with my

Own tender hands.

I know for myself, and I don't
need to prove

That I can create a world of
my own.

# Clarity

Oh, mighty lords, thy strength I deserve,

My blood I have made pure,

From my brow, my desires trickle,

Deliver me from evil.

For I shall not be tempted,

My body now shall be a temple for me

In which I shall reside

To beget the glory

Of my soul.

# A Dream

It's one of those days again...

No matter how hard I try

Can't seem to keep you

Off my mind...

The heart beats a thousand

Times,

Every second seems

To hold endless miles...

To have you close to me,

Of the things, I would like

You to say to me...

Do I keep it to myself,

Or share it with the skies above...

A day would be enough,

As if it never existed,

Then maybe it would fit well

Into the puzzle...

Is it momentary, would I want it

For eternity,

Of that, I am still

Unsure...

For its only me who's talking...

Maybe if I hear what's on your mind,

It would have the sway to

Change the whirlpools in my sea...

Would it be like a perfect painting,

Or would it again be a missed opportunity...

The uncertainty is enough,

To keep my feet sticking to the ground...

So, all I do is just close my eyes

And there you are smiling,

As you hold me and pull me

Into your dream...

The moist eyes

No shoulder to cry

Despair in its wings

The bird caught in a fire...

The whole world

Against its light

Nothing more to be said

Nothing more to be done

Silently it carries on. The unsung heroes

That lost the war...

The white flag now raised

What if the dove won't fly

Need to whisper into ears

These are just phases

Of time...

Dreams are lived

Dreams are broken

Some more are made. For whose hearts

Are made of gold...

So, worry not,

Need to fly

In the direction of the wind...

You've just forgotten,

How good it felt to carry on...

Now raise your head,

And soar to the skies...

Home will be home...

No questions asked ...

Life is but a dream...

The journey makes it

Worthwhile...

# The Doppelgänger

You know who I met?

The better part of yourself...

You said to me, you'll have to choose between the mind
and reality...

I said, what kind of question is that?

The brighter *you* said –

You deserve to be happy and not be

Caught in between the tragedy...

He looks just like you, he has the same memories as
you,

The flare for words just like yourself...

But he talks in a language much different than you,

He is what I need him to be...

Unlike you, never having enough words,

Not like you, depriving me of the kindness of
reciprocating gestures,

Unlike you, always waiting for me to start a
conversation...

Not like you, taking without offering and justifying
your ways...

Somewhere I want to believe you are the one calling me...

But then I think a fantasy you is so much better

Than the painful version of yourself...

I don't have to keep trying to make sense of things,

You understand every part of me...

I don't have to force you to be in a good mood,

It's you who takes me close and says, how do you do...

You're the yang that completes my yin,

And finally, maybe now I can go back to my usual
self and

Say to the reality of you Adieu,

Finally, I can rest in peace for I have found that part
of you

That will help me heal...

# Potions

Friendship is a potion in which

The key ingredients of trust,

Understanding, freedom and care have to be

Present but can be changed in

Proportion to suit your taste.

# Shadows

People say morals and values are

Building blocks of life;

Treasure, by protecting them with your

Own life;

Let them bring pain and sorrow but

The right must be done

But what good is right when wrong

Is the other.

Following the shadow may not lead

You to the person

But by following the person you

Will always see his shadow.

Morals and values are the shadows

Of humanity, which will always be

With you when the light is bright;

Without light, you cannot see a

Person,

So where will you see the shadows

Of beauty.

# The Adventure

This one's different,

Trying to Centre the gravity this time around me,

To ground me so that I am weaned from the fantasies...

A need to be heard, to share, to find the

Wavelengths that would attune to my depths,

So many lessons learnt,

How do I even begin to write and comprehend,

A feat that no amount of dedication would apprehend,

So, I look around me,

The mundane things representing the chaos,

The knots that I am trying to set free.

It's so much better when I just close my eyes,

See the world that I wish to thrive in,

Until the moments where it starts to devour me,

And then I come here to the limbo,

Where things seem uncertain, the fear creeping under
my skin.

The restless nights, a symptom or just a matrix

That I am trying to solve, to give me a sense of purpose.

These words will fade into the unknown,

The ashes blowing peacefully once their

Living is done.

I see it now, want to anchor,

Amid the things I have found,

But then the waves sweep over it,

The scene made perfect, oblivious of the

Fin I may have seen,

Telling me to rest assured and enjoy the evening.

It's a beautiful thing, you trying to make sense of

A hidden world...

You are so curious because you want to protect yourself,

Be ready and prepared

So that you aren't caught offhand,

The guards that shield up within your mind,

The beautiful gates with intricate carvings,

Cryptic, waiting to be unfolded by someone

Who will be all worth it,

But it's time you allow the rays to enter,

Sunshine will definitely do you some good,

The higher your towers,

You'll need dragons and shining armours,

But land your feet on the lush green grass,

Right outside your door and it's only then

A real adventure will have begun.

I see it now, want to anchor, here and now,

But then the waves sweep over it,

The scene made perfect, oblivious of the

Fin I may have seen,

Telling me to rest assured and enjoy the evening.

In the end no matter how many ways you devise to protect the self,

You would never be successful in stopping yourself

From getting extinguished,

No matter how much you try to understand,

The dimensions would always be infinite.

You can try and find one equation that fits it all,

But there will always be new frontiers that

Will require a reshuffling of the things you know.

What purpose is then left, but to accept all that you are Now.

# The Grit

Nothing,

I don't feel a thing...

The river swept away the anguish,

While you stood there choosing

To pull out the one from drowning...

It's a wonder I learnt to swim,

Didn't know whirlwinds

Can gift you steady fins...

I look back, it seems it was only a dream,

A nightmare that no longer hears screams...

The words don't stir me somehow,

There was a time I had gone on knees,

But not anymore...

It's not for me, it's not for me...

That life wasn't meant for me...

I have battled my demons, I am still

Standing...

The whispers do reach me, but

I tell them if they can't be loud,

They shouldn't bother me,

With their sound...

It's only me that I can hear,

When I look up at the sky now,

Everything seems crystal clear...

The desires have turned into

Indomitable Grit...

The vehemence has catalyzed into

Boreal warmth...

# IV

## LEAVING A MARK

# The Warrior

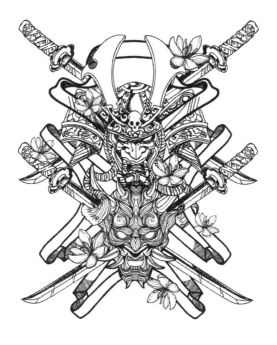

"I see your weakness, and I can't stay still, I'll be your shield, whose strength would be worthy, to withstand fire, of even the mightiest dragons.

I am fierce as justice awaits to be served in battles, chronicling victories that are to come. Courage is unbridled as I forge a sword to slay the fears,

I churn a weapon even out of the nimblest of metals. a way I find by mastering my mind, body and will."

# The Emerald

The depth & width of Gatsby's vision,

The Constellations of my

Imaginations dwelling,

So grand, it would

Belittle the bravest soul,

The child with an imagination

So vivid, where he would fight

Even destiny's charades...

The rotten crowd,

My worth the whole bunch

Put together...

The extraordinary gift of hope,

A gift that would never be

Found in any other person...

The verses of the story,

Etched on Belgium glass...

The finest glories that awaited

After rewriting the past...

But what good are

Letters, words, deeds,

To the likes of cowards,

Who turns their backs,

Careless people,

Who retreat into their shells,

At the first sign of doubt...

They would leave you in a lurch,

Use other's words to Survive,

While you close your eyes

With only one name on your lips...

Even then, there is no respite...

But still, the world ends,

Not for the cowards,

But the ones who carried

The Emerald light...

In that their innocence will

Decorate the magnificent casket...

With the silence of the night.

# Dream again

Hearts of wonder with swords of strength,
Even brighter thy vision of earth,
Come see the night has brought,
Darkness not but the peace of
Thy Kingdom that shall come...

# Cold Feet

It's not one of those love poems,

But just a few lines or so...

Can't explain this restlessness in my heart,

Do I feel it for you...or some unknown scar...

I have been trying to reason...

But can't seem to rest my mind and heart,

So I thought I would write a few lines...

Do you think it would be wrong...

It's been a while now,

I tried all I could to distract myself.

Have gone through a lot of ups and a hell of downs to know this

The feeling is temporary...

But still, it makes me smile,

Makes me alive, to live a full life.

To err is but human,

But I intend not to play with anyone's strings...

It's just a pure phase in life,

Not knowing what may lie ahead,

Knowing what I may miss out on,

Or what I might gain...

This mind is a curious thing,

It knows not sometimes where it treads,

But I know I am true,

And there won't be a doubt no more...

For this is not a poem of fantasy,

But it's as real as it gets,

That there are a few unknowns,

To an equation of life,

Divide, multiply, add or subtract,

It will lead me finally to a

Fraction or a whole...

And I intend to find my way through

The rough columns of time.

# Strings Attached

Have been so scared of the cravings,

Thinking they have the magic to sniff life into puppet strings ...

But the fear lies not in the will but

The fact, of what if the dreams are fulfilled...

Then it dawned... That is not what I want...

It's only the fractions of you that I long...

Only the role and not the character...

Only the best parts, not the disasters...

I have put up with enough catastrophes,

And they cut so deep that no more

Can I indulge in killing myself softly...

Now I want only the sterling parts,

The gratification without expectations,

The smiles and laughter without the tears,

The ice cream without the melting...

You, without all the bullshit...

I want to ruin you, for once I too was forsaken...

And now it only seems like a fair chance...

Nurture you only to devour you raw...

Hold you now only cause I am lost...

If I cared, wouldn't have I behaved well...

But no, though intentions were genuine,

There are splinters which won't cut the dark ...

So be on your way, and don't look back,

For there is nothing here but

Desires that have no intentions of

Strings being attached...

# The Cure

So much has changed,

And still, some remains the same...

The same flowered sheets,

The same identical mirror,

The ceiling fan that creeks

The drawers that hide the laundry,

The posters of captured moments,

The pictures of realities lived...

Is it just me, or has the place

Shrunk to its normal size...

I feel like myself,

More within my skin

As I wake up on my own accord,

No fear to please others,

No hurry to cook a meal,

The same chores feel lighter,

As the obligations have,

Seemed to have disappeared...

So much has happened in these years...

The one who was scared and reaching out,

Appears to be writing words

Of making sense of all the things around,

The nights that were longed for and the

Mornings that were dreaded,

Seem a bit calmer now...

Not desperate anymore,

Took a lot to pick up the sands of time,

A lot of tears, fears and anger...

The shame of bearing the soul,

Has blossomed into the courage

To take a stand...

But still, the heart is fretted,

There seems to be no cure

For certain things...

Oh, all means were tried,

But all that could be done was to,

Dilute the potion into tangerine...

But it still doesn't follow the laws

Of physics,

The fear of being rejected and abandoned,

Have their roots deep within...

Can't resort to writing prose anymore,

So the technique of finding an

Alternative response,

Is to summarize the feelings

Into poetry...

Need to keep the thoughts at bay,

The Tsunamis at a distance,

Are just the crests and troughs,

Need to remind myself,

This time I won't lose them forever...

# The Change

People change and so do you

With time and waves passing through life,

It does not matter who you are it does not matter who you become

As long as you are satisfied with

What you have become.

People will love you at a

Specific phase and if you change then

So, will they.

You will love someone for a particular thing

And maybe they too for some reason they find in you,

However, when seasons change so will everything;

But you will find that special someone

Who will fall in love with your change of course,

And if it is meant to be so will you,

And you will be in love for many seasons to come.

# The Blue Whale

It's an unfair world, a lesson taught to all,

A calf and a cub, except the human condition...

That's what makes it so difficult to accept

That what's gone can never again be touched...

This is how one describes despair...

This is how the encumbrance and vexation of care are felt...

Never has a moment gone by in the world

That someone hasn't felt these words...

So what do you do?

How much deeper in the mine can you get...

Have you forgotten there is no future but only the present...

An illusion so divine, it's stronger than any opium that you might find...

But you still go ahead and stretch out your Palm...

You still rouse every morn...

For your time has not yet come...

There is still more pain to be felt...

There is always more happiness to be gained...

And that is all that keeps you awake.

For in the end...

Fear seems to evaporate...

And all that you are left is with a single breath...

So wake up... Don't do your best...

It's all going to go to waste...

Instead, just open your eyes and be delectable

That you still can see your own hands about to make beautiful mistakes...

For happiness has been overrated...

It is through the pain that the most glorious smiles are awakened...

Can you feel it in your veins,

The rhythm of the blood singing to your fame...

It's only when you're not pale

That you can feel the luxury of an affliction...

It's only when you're sad...

You realize what it meant to be fragrantly mesmerized...

So despair all you want...

Feel the depths of the ocean which you can never surmount.

For in that consternation you will realize...

An astounding magnificent

Blue Whale is what you have become...

For how many can claim to have seen a creature

So rapturous in the dawn or dusk...

# The Demon Vanquished

Never thought I would feel this way,

Still amazed, can see my own self astonished

By the calm, I feel inside my head.

His voice or his call to my loved one,

Didn't seem threatening,

Is it because now I finally feel safe?

My mind I can silently see churning,

Trying to find ways in which it can still

Surprise me, alert me, let me know I need to

Fear something.

But there is this part of me,

Which doesn't seem to be bothered anymore.

Is this really me?

Or is it something I am repressing ...

Can I finally smile and realize that I have had my victory?

Is full victory really possible?

Have I ended all the karmic bonds?

I am feeling like testing my spirits...

Maybe another name that disturbs me,

Maybe life is still throwing things at me...

But surprisingly I have learnt the tricks of the trade,

The compassion I have shown myself,

Has it really worked its magic?

My immunity seems to be in full glory,

Is this how it's supposed to be,

I feel I don't need to try so hard anymore,

Just keep up my healthy diet,

And the White Knights will do their job,

Effortlessly, I need to trust my army.

To protect me from all the foreboding and inhumanity.

The past seems to have been dealt with,

The present doesn't seem to have the threat anymore,

The anticipation of a possible war in the future does seem to hold sway,

But I think I will handle it in any which way.

Or die trying, till I know I have stood up and survived as long as I have lived...

And it's been glorious without any regret.

# The Waves

My feet sink in the sand a little,

Just enough to wiggle my toes,

The first time I have managed to stay on the shore,

Still uncertain will I be able to hold in the urge to

Dive into the water.

It would have been a great adventure if I had

A boat with sails of silver, an anchor to watch the
sunset,

As the Gannets flew across the horizon.

But I often find myself taking a plunge in stormy seas,

Oblivious of the impending squall & the whirlpools

In which I have been caught numerous times.

Still, I don't know how I have found myself on this
islands shore,

Hadn't expected to survive the freezing troughs.

I take a step back as the wave tries to kiss my feet,

Afraid that the sand beneath would move my stead.

But then again, I take two steps forward to

Just test the waters to see if I am ready.

I am long away from home,

Not even knowing if I would find a way back

To a fireplace that would warm up my bones.

Sitting in front of it, with a quilt weaved of the goodness in a heart;

Along with a red wine filled glass.

I wiggle my toes to remind myself,

This time I won't swim against the tide,

I'll wait for Cassiopeia to show me the way.

# The Eclipse

Every time I reach out, against all odds...

As if stuck in loops time and again,

No good ever came of it.

The abandonment lived through the illusions we see.

You managed to hurt me just as much.

Little time, I do not have anymore.

Years have passed,

And no regret and guilt will make things right,

I am aware of that now.

You have become too used to living a life

Detached...

Your reasons may be the noblest,

But I can't follow you like a pup anymore.

Wait on you till you are ready...

For you want to keep flying to escape the

Reality,

While I have no wings, only four paws.

A life you have lived without me in it,

You have survived, just as much...

Too used to, you have been, with making your

Peace for having lost everything,

Losing me thus doesn't seem much,

For you have lost far too much.

I on the other hand, never let anything

Slip, kept it collected with all my might,

Even when my hands fell short.

But I guess now I need to stop these futile

Attempts...

Alice in Wonderland had her Mad Hatter,

For me, I don't need to be distressed in my

Wonderland...

I will also find my solace and learning to

let go of the need for you.

I don't even have to tell you anything,

Just disappear into the rabbit hole,

But I do share I do speak, thinking

Am morally obliged.

My silly mind telling me that maybe

You might wither away without me,

A false sense of Ego eluding me.

Never seeing that there is a possibility,

That I don't have to live with this

Pain anymore.

I do not owe you anything,

Nor do you to me.

Let me just walk away from the sunset,

Aeons have passed me standing there,

Now my legs and heart have turned numb.

Doesn't matter even if you smile or not

Anymore.

That smile has lost its power to

Regain the faith that I had once.

My imagination needs to move out of

The eclipse of your sacrifice,

Under your shadow, all I have

Done is prospered outwardly as I

Felt hollower inwardly.

Trying to fill the spaces, with the

Idea of unconditional love,

Coming to realizations that,

All I had to deal with were conditions,

A little more time,

A bit of acceptance,

A bit more distance,

A bit of restraint.

And all I had was conditional love.

It's time... The season is changing,

And so is my heart, wanting to

Escape the burdens of your

Sacrifice.

My pyre will burn someday.

But you won't hold the log

That will set fire to the rain.

I have done enough,

You have done enough.

Time to let go of the blame,

The guilt for having moved on,

Then for luring you to what you desire,

The criminality for wanting you again,

For making you dependent on my faith,

The culpability for having been ready to leave it all,

For not being there for you when you needed me

The most,

For choosing to stay friends even when I wanted more,

The guilt for embarrassing ourselves,

For making you lose out on friends.

For promising you things which now I can't fulfil,

The blame for wanting to commit sins,

Hovering in me like a dark cloud,

For not having left the world for you.

But was it really all my fault?

That's an answer we both know

Will never be enough.

You too will write a poem,

Where in I'll be the eclipse and the sunshine,

For me now,

No poem will ever have your mention in it.

Too many words have flown like the sea,

And I never was able to seep through the

Mountains to reach the other side.

I only crashed against the rocks,

Which broke the waves of my trust.

It's time I flow unapologetically like

I should have a long time ago.

That's how you have taught me to be.

So, don't fear to lose me now.

You lost me bit by bit each day,

When you chose to say No.

Doesn't seem to matter anymore,

The Alchemy is rewinding to balance

Out the harmony.

I now feel a sense of peace in my heart.

Now I know why you were so persistent

To not let go of your Solace.

It's good to return to your inner core &

Shut out the voices and embrace the silence

That you have longed for.

# Birthday

A smile you added to my life

And made my days happier,

To God, I ask the same

To give you all the happiness

You ever dreamed.

Let each day pass by, knowing

You are the one who made the day,

Let the time wait to know,

That you are the one who made it wait

To realize that you are the man who

Can save the day and make it

So wonderful that each day will say

I want to be your Birthday.

So many wonders you hold in your heart

You yourself do not know,

What strength you have will be seen

By the hearts of others.

You can soar high above in the sky

Or go deep within the sea,

But you will always be a diamond

Which shines in the sky or sea...

Also, they say that beauty lies

In the eyes of the beholder

So, don't you ever change for only loving

Eyes can see beauty.

This is all I can say

With a big HAPPY BIRTHDAY.

# Shimmering Light

Shimmering light, facing the dark

Seeks the cuts to make a mark

Hope he brings into the world where

Justice rules only it is to bring

Balance into these not so random stars,

The change shall come; change shall go,

Things will be undone to make tomorrow grow,

But Constance there will lie, to bring a tear

To the weaker side,

Constance will come,

Constance will shimmer,

To bring the courage to know and act,

tears are to be undone, to build a sword,

You shall fall into the water

At the step that it holds,

Let it cleanse you not drown,

Fear not the step but learn to draw...

Shimmering light on the sword so fine

Shimmering light on the water so light

Shimmering light on the stars that make you dream...

# The Wizard

"I see you sighing, and all I want to do is say the spell, which would make your wishes come true. The laws that make up the universe is the parable that intrigues me. There is much more than meets the eye. I can bend and break fates by the slight of my hand, making you think am devious but am the one who weaves the dream catchers to keep the nightmares at bay. Travesties I abhor for that's not how I play cards; Everything is a balance, equal parts of giving and taking.

Come on now, let's make things happen, I do not eye the crown, for,

I am the one true Kingmaker."

# The Surf

From the clothes to your soul...

The changes are magnificent,

Drowning out the voices,

Of all the prejudices...

Making you into more than

What you have been...

All it takes is two souls that,

Inherit one body...

It's been a Surf,

To go through the crest and troughs of life...

Keeping up with the traditions and still finding

Independence to have a spine...

Having to say some difficult goodbyes,

The roots have been shaken with the earthquake

Of foreboding and ruse...

But still, we take in the breath to remind us of what we can be...

Gratitude seems like the hope,

Swaying on the blades of grass...

Like opium awaiting to seek its course...

The things you learn are not just taught in class...

We don't always work with our heart or mind...

But there is something beyond the realms of time...

And everything seems worth it

When love transcends the quantum of existence ...

# Words

Words fail to say what you mean

Are they be supposed to ease your pain

Are they to be spoken to go unheard

Unspoken when they are only to be heard louder

If not you still will be unheard

A stone can't be moved without magic words,

Is magic the path to the unreal

Cave or the way to a beautiful world

So much is to be shared to show a rope,

To be said to make a bow

Stones are shattered when they go unheard.

A wall is to be raised

When there is no end to the road

Words fail to say what you mean

Words fail, to make you scream, to
make you clean...

# Eyes of Stone

Eyes of stone thou can't see

The pain that has been brought upon me.

I do not know if I would

Love you for time to come,

My own love, I can't trust.

You did show me the world of beauty

But even as I try hard to love you,

The thought of betrayal stops me,

So now I must find my own way

For the things, I must do,

For my own days.

# The Fatal Flaw

A tempest wreaking havoc amidst the mind,

How would you detail this picturesque vibe?

Would you burn the charcoal even more?

To get a darker shade of black?

Would you bleed blood at the edge of a steel cliff...

Would you drown yourself in the

melancholic ambience of beauty and potent sedatives,

Would you growl and rip apart everything that
surrounds you?

Wish there was a lever to pull down on,

To shut one's supply off before any harm is done,

To stop the short circuit

That was the cause of eventually the house burning...

There seems to be a fatal flaw in the way we are
designed,

Can't seem to say the things we want when we have the
time.

Too late the realization dawns of what has been done,

But can you really blame your own self for a cognitive
distortion?

If everyone around you lied and mocked you,

How can you differentiate between who is to be trusted and,

Whose intentions were to protect you,

Wild with rage you set fire to the rain,

Tears seem too weak a mechanism if you are to stand up again,

You regret then the good deeds for one feels alienated,

In the tryst to differentiate between right and wrong,

You stumble upon the words written which seem like

The perfect melody you had been trying to hum...

It then melts that stone-cold facade,

To let in some ray of light, on your guards to

Shut back, even the sight of the slightest rejected smile.

You then look around you, now that your back,

The mess that has been made by a fatal flaw.

It couldn't have been you, who has ravaged every inch

Of what was once a shrine you prayed to,

The place you looked for when nothing made sense to you.

Where do you now go to ask for forgiveness,

What do you even say?

No, the fault hasn't been with you,

It does take two to make that swirl across the ballroom.

Everything has been said and done,

Time again you have built something from scratch and

Watched it fall like a house of cards in rhythm...

Every word you write still seems a

Failed attempt to try and explain your side,

How do you reach out when the door

Was not even kept open wide,

How do you reach out when all the signs

Were made to make you believe

Your direction was misaligned.

Which way do you go when you keep

Stumbling on your own shadow, You stay mad, and you let go,

All this was not a Fatal flaw, I want to believe, maybe Someday despite everything,

Every Scar, Every mark would have meant something.

Isn't it said that the imperfections are what add to the beauty,

But I'll know what you'll say,

These aren't imperfections they are fatal flaws

& I don't want anything to do with it.

So, I turn back, wanting to hold my head high,

The churning in my chest is making me dizzy

But I won't ask for your help.

I'll just walk for a while and find that perfect bench,

With a view of a pond and children playing to my left,

And to the right, I'll have the ice cream truck,

I'll finish my cone in a hope one day you'll

Buy me the next one without judging me how

Flawlessly I managed to smile no matter the
contusions.

# I Am Therefore I Think

The cat caught my tongue

When I realized you meant me

And I meant you...

Me time, your time... Time and Again,

Destined to keep fighting Again...

But I still can't find the perfect words...

Too far to reach the cord now invisible...

But like always the silly girl...

Failing to realize what you mean...

Jumping to conclusions, trying to protect myself from the imaginary

Stone you might cast at me...

But all your doing is trying to have a conversation with me...

I don't forget the cravings, have never taken anything for granted...

I Don't have all the answers...

All I just meant, which you failed to

Decipher is... I felt alone when

There was no one, and I still feel alone even with everyone...

A malady I wish someone had the solution for...

Cause I'm too tired to keep

Figuring out if, 'I think, therefore I am.'

Or 'I am therefore I think.'

I shall find my own way...

Through the darkness and light...

First, there was darkness, and I was just a child...

Now the light is so bright that I feel like a Bat without its Sonar...

But the dusk and dawn are the best times of the day...

The perfect light to set things right...

# 21 Days

I thought to myself...

21 days it takes to change a habit...

How do I make it worthwhile,

These days of grace that have

Caused the whole earth to stop for a while...

The pets would be happier to have their masters home,

The children ecstatic with no rules of schools to follow,

Little do they know, their parents would shower on them,

Their anxieties and fear...

In a bid to make sense of the uncertainty spanning

So close to the threshold...

21 days, how do I build a difference,

Could this be an opportunity to try something different...

No more competing with Exotic selfies,

Everyone has been humbled down, within the four walls of their home,

No more trying hard to make excuses, to keep the hurtful ones at bay,

But what do we do if we have been quarantined

With the ones who are hard to tolerate...

Do we once again delve to the world of fantasy,

What if I told you the broom could be your answer to everything...

Witches you see travelled on them far and wide,

Warlocks envied the magic that potion and herbs conjured,

Within the kitchen as pots and pan did their dancing...

The Alchemy that churned when you experimented

With the resources, you had at hand,

They turned to chants and music to cast the most powerful spells...

To make you value all that you now seem to have taken for granted ...

Yoga and work from home look like the new Mantra...

21 days, How do I make the most of it...

I think I'll just sit back and try to find my soul...

I think I'll let words be my company,

This time I know I am safe, no one can get after me,

In my own solace, I will pray not to the lords,

But for the grace of having made this far...

How would the title to a book sound now that

Superstition and life hack forwards are giving rumours, new authors...

How would love stories now bloom with, no gatherings or holy communes,

The title would be –

Love in the Times of Coronavirus instead of Cholera…

Am not the only one alone anymore,

Each one now left to their own device,

Would they find the method to this madness?

Only time would tell…

This could be a real gateway for some alien holiday,

No one they would find roaming the streets,

If it was some kind of invasion am sure it would

Ends like Tom Cruise's War of Worlds…

A Third World War seems befitting if

This is some kind of a Biological weapon…

Elon Musk then would be the one with the Lightsaber,

Lookout, lookout,

You better not mess with us, dear Darth Vader…

The world will go back to its old ways …

But I have these days where I will always remember what it felt,

To realise there is much more to life than the rat race.

Do we scout for stocking up food climbing over each other's back,

Or does the frustration peak as we are told not to cross the Laxman Rekha…

Do we despair for all the things we do not have,

No ration in the closet, it makes it hard to find the rationale

For everything that's been happening...

But again, haven't you always complained,

For not having enough time,

Now no more excuses as the

Will to do something is right at the palm of your hands...

You did long for the world to change a bit,

There you have it,

A pandemic is what came along,

Not to raise havoc as the apocalypse suggested

But instead made you take it easy and

Urged you to stay indoors...

The stocks may be bearish,

Leading to an economic depression,

But the Corona Din will eventually

Boost morale once it's all over...

Such a small tiny virus, what it can do when it multiplies,

It has the capacity to divide the entire human tribe...

The mass hysteria reminding me of the Salem witch trials...

But again we thought we were the ones doing nature a favour,

Not realizing that Mother Earth has her ways of bringing a balance,

We are but mere children, who thought we could save her,

but she knows when to set things in order

When things get over the border...

This disease of the rich,

Has given the art of war new found technicalities,

The poor have always known what hunger could do,

This time Karma has found a way to

Show hoarders what happens when

You get too used to stealing what doesn't belong to you...

It could be a great time to set things right

With all the sore relationships. An excellent time to see who

Can be reliable & trustworthy while wearing the N95...

With these words, I take a bow, I have yet to have dinner, would you like to join in for some wine & cauliflower on Google Duo ?...

# The Making

I will make people want to dream

Is what I had said to a dear friend once...

A continuum which made me feel so strong

That my mind and heart set to make it come true...

But HOW? Is the question I am left with...

How can something as little as I make an urge

So strong that would open doors for others

Which they have not even seen?

Fear of the unknown, now I feel is the lock

Whose key I need to find

To open the doors of chance for me...

But again, how to find a key

When everything that surrounds you

Is an answer to something...

Should I be like the wind unseen yet powerful

Or the earth persevering and humble

Or like the water precocious and adjustable

Like the fire warm but fierce??

But now the question that rises is WHAT instead

Of a *How,* so should we look deeper

Into the lock than the key?

It's not the answers that hold an answer

But questions themselves...

How will I make people dream?

Dissolve the fear to dream of being better,

To open your mind to the most magnificent

Thing you can ever think or imagine of and

Have no fear of loss, because what lies ahead

No one knows, so why to give in to the fear of the unknown,

Just ask the universe, which is out there,

Instead of wishing upon a star just try

Hoping for your own sun...

It's not luck that's God's gift to you but

Your choice and positive thinking that

God or the force or energy whatever you may call,

Could have blessed you with to make all your

Wishes would come true, Believe in it, have faith in it...

Now I know it's not others but me who wants

Myself to dream...to dream without the fear

Of the unknown, like the open sky, I will

Form shapes and colours and when someone

Just looks at me they will see what

Power can lie within, they will feel and see

What they want, for each cloud has a different shape,

And the same colour holds different meanings...

So, I will dream.

# The Rebel

"I see you broken, and I can't take it anymore, will go against
the world if that's what it takes to make sense of it all,

Hell hath no fury as a heart scorned, You can call it revenge
or a revolution, I will turn the tides all in my favour,

If they outcast me I have not a care in the world, without a
flinch, I'll give them a taste, of their own medicine,

History now shall be written with pen alchemized into arrows."

# Land of My Own

Ups and downs

I have gone through,

Love and hate

I have felt,

What more can I ask this world,

What more can I say to this world,

When what I want cannot be done

Only be done in my dreams.

Nothing is left for me to see

In this beautiful world,

Nothing is left for

Closing my eyes to, in this pitiful world.

I seek no pot of gold nor

A bowl of pleasure.

How will I now fly into the sky that I can see,

How will I reach the coastline I can feel?

Walking into the kingdoms unknown how

Will I find the land of my own.

# Losing Myself

The world I see

Is different from what others might see,

For the things I know, I see through them.

Their very existence bewilders me,

Makes me think what they are,

Making my sane turn insane.

The world I know I should see with an open mind,

But the world how others see I can't find.

It pushes me down to be so different,

It drives me up to think so beautifully.

This way is stopping me from...

This way is taking me away from

Finding myself from within a hole.

# Still Nowhere

How does one get a message delivered one thinks to herself,

It's a silly thing to be worrying about this with all that is there,

Newspapers, Blogs, Sms's, Calls, Snail mail and E-mail,

This world has come so close, it's become so easy to share your woes...

But still, there seems to be a void,

People still can't seem to decide,

So much has already been said and done, but it isn't enough...

You hear about it every day,

It's a curse to be born that way,

A tear drops each and every single day...

Charity they say starts at home,

But it's a pity we don't follow that as our own,

We are taught so many things;

We grow up with these silly things,

Someone is weak;

Someone is strong even when their heart is one,

Someone is pure,

Someone profane even when they are beneath the same sun,

Someone always gets to say a yes while the other stays mum,

Even when it's a choice that is to be given to all.....

One doesn't know if she is saying it right,

She can't just make the words to fight,

It's such a simple thing, so widely known,

but it's still so difficult to make sense of it all,

All now one can say is that

We need to start with an unusual subject at school,

To unlearn all that we know –

The Myths about Women to Overcome the Superstition;

Because what we know seems to just make them miserable...

Science was supposed to make one progress,

Art was supposed to build one's heart and soul,

Informal education was supposed to make one smart,

But now if we go to think we haven't

Been able to solve women's problems,

Because the subject matter itself was taught all wrong...

Look at this new thing;

You don't have to name it because

It doesn't belong to any,

Look with a set of fresh eyes;

An encouraging plea just see;

It's every other thing that you see,

And then you will know,

That 'we' are no different from you oh mortals,

We too need a portal through which

We can walk to make a place of our own...

# The Patriarch

Even the attempt to name these lines with the title of
my choosing

Makes me twirl inside for all the audacious attempts
made to hurt my pride.

He builds a pack of sycophants with the alluring charm

of intellectual arrogance and trains his young
manipulating

And feeding off their empathy to compensate for his
own insecurities.

His mother made him the apple of her eye and

There stems the narcissism that would lead a generation

To dysfunctional familial cries.

If not that, then she failed to protect his sensitivities

From the man that shredded her for raising an unfit
child.

His wife he makes sure satisfies all his appetites

Especially where all her sense of individuality

Is mocked to only praise his virtuous, pious hypocritical
lullabies.

If she or her children dare not acknowledge

His attention-seeking self-glorifying avocations,

He will hold back his positive reinforcements and

Give them the silent treatment or then rain down
humiliating vocabulary.

It's mind warfare at play,

The whole of Society is the board that this game of
chess is played in.

The Good Samaritan is the name he goes by in public,

lauded for all the work he has done selflessly.

But if you look closely, none of the efforts can truly

Be attributed to him solely for its been his colleagues

And family who actually helped him achieve that
prestige.

A facade of humility is put on to show the world

How ethically upright he could be,

The help and kindness in his heart seem like an endless
ocean...

Even the ships that sail within will rarely realize

That it's a trap for if it doesn't suit his agenda or

The way he wants things to be,

He can devour everything even without a sincere
apology.

He would have high expectations

Of all that you must do,

Hit you below the belt if you dared to venture

A step away from his line of thought,

It then gets so suffocating when all his good deeds

Are showcased on the best walls of the room

While your efforts are swept under the rug

Making your existence inconsequential.

If you try to make his pack realize that their Alpha is actually rabid,

It will be met with denial and what they perceive

As unquestionable loyalty is the fear of abandonment

That has been instilled at a core

If they dared to even question his philosophy.

The wife, a mere puppet reduced to

The mentality of an immature child,

Chided with and made a fuss over as well as

Giving her the regular dose of punishment

If she misbehaved in any manner,

A neurotic whose jealousy and insecurity

Would be passed on to all the daughters

especially the ones that won't be hers.

The son will follow in the footsteps,

Always awaiting the validation and

Acceptance to be seen as a Man,

That would never come,

For his Being reduced only to a mere reminder

That he is the product of his loins and virility,

A reflection of himself,

No matter how hard that self would try to mirror

The master all he would get is the dismissal

And abject denial of what he can never be.

Then one fine day there comes a cub

Unsure of her place and pack,

She takes the role of a lamb,

Best suited as she longs to be loved and accepted

For the horrors that already befell her.

At first, gratitude filled her heart

For having found a pack that took her in,

So, she did her best to fit in.

But when it started to mould her into

Something she could never be,

When it began to remind her of the horrors she already
had escaped from,

Where the same allegations and attacks

Had made her whimper and curl into a corner,

Where no cries of help were heeded to but

Met with outright denial and the falsified truth,

Something stirred in her soul.

Deep down inside her dark core,

Something moved,

She still couldn't figure out the knot

That was entangling her even more,

Finally, she took the pen and stabbed it right into

Each one of their minuscule hearts.

Covered in blood,

Finally, she turned her back and left the scene,

All that was left was a birth

That would change her reality and

No more could she ever be reduced

To a lamb that was actually a Man Eater

With canines that would hunt anyone

Coming near her shore.

# Fairness

No one gets what they deserve,

Not the tears or the smile...

Things are done...

You beg you cry they can't be undone

Nor made right...

Things are done...

You laugh, you know... Life will still go on...

With a darkness within you,

With the light that you want to find...

# Blessings and Curses

What good are curses when you know they won't
work...

What good is a sunrise if it can't be seen who needs it
the most,

What good is death if it doesn't come for people who
have no need to live,

What good is rain if it can't wash away a tainted soul...

Of all the things He has created,

I don't think of him as a painter,

And indeed, if he is then,

One may think he just didn't put his heart in the
picture,

How can he just watch, how can he just let it be?

And am sure it is a He,

For all the burden has been made to be carried by a she;

She needed an indestructible heart to face all the
sacrifices,

But he gave her a one, so fragile that it always has to
break,

She needed strength to bear all the pain;

She needed more to build a bridge,

But all she was given were weaknesses,

Hungry vultures would circle above always as she walked on her way...

It's not fair to be made so helpless,

There is no court in nature,

Just a mythical hell and heaven...

What good will it do to curse our fellows,

They are but a part of nature's cult,

This way of life is so cold; it's such a pity,

Humans weren't given wings to just fly away from danger...

But then it is said this life is to prepare you for a better flight,

But what good is retribution when you don't know your crime,

What good is pain if happiness is as elusive,

As a mirage in hot planes...

But again, they say, life is what you make of it,

It's all in your mind the rain and snow,

But if this is true why then does it hurt,

Even when you don't want it to,

Why do tears come even when you wipe them with your own fingers...

Any way you choose people will still prove you wrong,

I don't understand how they can be so far away from their own home,

Even if there is a noble dream to make tomorrow a better day,

The drops that fall are too small,

Will take too long to fill this ocean with its waves...

What good is a smile when you know it will never remain,

What good are stars when clouds seal their fate,

What good is the sky when you can't feel it or fly,

What good is music if it reminds you of the past,

What good is a sunset if it won't take you to the other side,

What good is this life without the love that was meant to shine...

# Into the Night

Feel like giving you a piece of my mind,

Even though I know it makes me vulnerable

As you give your snarling smiles...

The bruises you give me,

With those

Invisible knives,

Sugar coating your selfish needs under innocent
smiles...

I often wonder, what would happen to you,

If you were ever put into my two shoes,

Then would your towering arrogance,

See the humility of the thousand shed pearls,

And would you still then give that unknowing smile,

Not a day would you last,

Would have given up

A Longtime back ...

For never will you dare to tread the water that lurks
within me,

For that courage, you have lost in the midst of your

Protected shield …

You'll ask a hundred times, of what went wrong,

And no amount of words can ever suffice the

Unintelligent glance…

Lack of empathy, crowned by the haughty resilience…

It's nothing but aloofness,

Coated with artificial benevolence…

May it be gaslighting,

Or patronizing behaviours,

Or double standards coupled with a pinch of narcissism…

Now I know where the bitterness emanates from…

It's the torn eyelids with which now the future and past encompass,

For gone are those sweet dreams,

A mere reflection of what was meant to be.

For the promises have been worn out by time,

As you sleep by into the night.

# Letting Go

Of all the things that I have seen,

Of all the things I have felt,

It's like stones being tied to my hand and feet,

With my mouth stuffed with rotting cloth,

Someone just pushed me into the depths of the ocean unknown,

I fear it is me, who has let myself drown,

With this disease that eats me up,

I fear it is them, who pushed me down when I needed help,

With this, I cry out to them, but no one would hear me,

Instead, they poke and push me with sticks and knives,

So that I bleed and won't call out to them...

The sun seems to have set,

with no one beside me under these depths,

I think of all the ones who must have drowned,

In these forsaken depths, I see bubbles as I fall below,

But they won't reach the surface, now am too far below,

I fight; I fight so hard to set myself free,

To swim to the shore once where

I had walked with no care in the world,

I fight; I wriggle to get myself out of the chains,

I can hear them rattling but now

It's been long since they started rusting,

I had thought the saltwater would erode the rocks, making them lighter,

But all I see is that more moss has collected, making them strong...

I think to myself maybe I am better here,

I shouldn't complain, what happens, is always some kind of gain,

It's a miracle no shark has come to make things worse...

I can see the marks on my hands and feet,

The scars that are still fresh seem to be inviting more troubles,

I see so many monsters nibbling at my skin,

That I feel now, it would have been better if I had been killed...

I see sunlight and console myself,

Maybe someone could see me and come for help,

Then I think to myself, it's such a weakness to be so dependent,

God helps those who help themselves,

So, I rattle my chains again and try to cut them by the rocks,

Soon I see a ray of hope, the one for which I had waited for so long,

I think all these things have built up character,

Whatever happens, never goes in vain,

But just as I am about to get free,

I see a shark coming at me, Then I think to myself,

"When I had wished for you, oh creature,

Why did you not come, and now when I am free

You come towards me with darkness in your heart"...

Then I hear a voice say to me,

"Ungrateful child how weak art thou,

I put in your mind the thought of hope,

I gave you life, you don't even know!

How grand a life I have planned for you,

Your nibbled skin was food for someone,

Your drowning was a lesson to you and all,

To know the good from bad, I have given you everything,

And yet you 'crib', you curse,

You should be thankful for all that has been done!"

So then with my rotting body, I face my Saviour,

But the shark too doesn't want me for I stink of old...

Are they even tears running down my cheek?

Or is it the ocean moving me against my will...

I don't know what more to say or ask,

I don't know what I did wrong, I don't know why I am here,

I don't know if it's the feeling or reality that is killing me slow...

# Just Once

You're my soulmate! The one I would die for! You're my love

The kind that happens just once!

Now tell me, doesn't that sound a little insane?

A little, just a little insane,

When this world is imagined having parallel worlds...

You can never ever feel the same...

Never can you feel the same touch again...,

For you live through the people, you touch...

You never die just once,

For you die each time, you lose someone's touch...

But let me tell you,

You can love again, again if you have lost your love...

For don't you heal back when you fall ill,

Don't you learn to live with scars of a healed wound?

Don't you love your friends even though they are more than one...?

So, you can fall in love again,

Just like lightning that has different volts,

But never does lightning fall at places with the same intensity,

So, you will have to choose when the time comes,

Because we aren't talking about

Multiple torrid affairs but of healing hearts...

Love can happen again only if you

Give yourself a fair chance to feel alive again...

# Confession

To a boy who I don't know why...

Had to say this to him,

For crazy things can be done just a numbered number of times...

Forbidden I know it is this path I have chosen

But in all the years that are still to come...

Why in fear should one live, it's not a sin

But a pure thought, just a message from a stranger... Please do keep this a secret...

For some dreams are never meant to be shared... I know not what truth lies within you,

Neither do I know what I have done is right or wrong... Forgiveness is all I can ask for, and words are all that I can give...

Nothing in return, I ask...

And now you shall never hear my voice again,

I am just a girl, no more can I do this again...

# Jungfrau

Purity is it a material form...

Is it to be retained for another's pleasure? ...

Can't we even have a right on what is our very own...

'Vir' is for man, 'Gin' is for a trap, quite a right pair it makes

To explain it all...

For history is written by the one who wins in war

Otherwise, it wouldn't have been Eve but Man himself

Who would have been made to bear the burden of beauty

If God was written to be a woman...

Purity lies not in our bodies but in our hearts,

Magic is performed not when hands touch

But when hearts meet...

We weep of blood, not for our sins but

We cry for our protectors, don't set us free...

# The Werewolf

It begins precisely on that day,

Near the first end of every moon phase,

The hackles raised, the mind blurs,

To the anticipated brawls that are to come,

She feasts on the moments captured in time,

From ancient ruins, thrones and secret waterfalls...

The Knight in the Shining armour that stabbed her

In the back. Now unsure of what he has brought forth...

In the cycles of the crescent and gibbous...

She won't spare him, till she tastes his blood

Soaked with elixir...

She shapeshifts from her docile, loyal form,

To bite her own master, for the lines now

Fade between fate and desire...

She dreads the moon, losing herself

To nature's ways...

No curses can tame her,

Threats are hay, beneath her prowling sleigh...

One look is enough, a smile tears through the

Silence, his feet fear, as she treads near...

What is it that draws her to her albatross,

She can't explain,

So easy it would be to just extinguish him,

Into the depths of time...

But all she wants would be,

To have him on his knees,

To undress his masks and

Bare his chest with his heart

On the tombstone where all the

Spells and promises are set free...

The stabbed knife pulled out,

He brings it to his human heart,

Piercing it deeply, his eyes begin to change form,

He becomes what she is, she in turn

Brushes her mane against his...

The thirst now will be unabridged,

The ritual now can be complete for

How far could each of them escape knowing

Wolves mate for life...

# The Spine

How amazing is the spine...

The bones of strength protecting

The vulnerabilities of the frail,

A network of threads that hold

The answers to evolutions most

Marvellous overheads...

Finally, in time, things seem to have

Unravelled to give a clue...

Have you ever wondered what it would Do,

To be without a spine to hold you...

The weight of the world would

Become so heavy, that one would give up Easily,

Cursing for they were not bestowed with

Even the basics of frugality ...

More difficult it is for the ones who live in their shadows,

For though they have been bequeathed with a brawny vine,

Others mock them while they sip their wine...

You try to grow into them,

To offer some Brace,

But then you realize, all you are left with is,

Memories that are hard to erase...

A stage comes when you start

Feeling the weight of their misgivings,

And be forewarned that they will make sure

That you know, you are all that they crave...

While they still deny you,

The sustenance that you conscientiously deserve...

It makes you grow weak,

Even if you think it's a great bargain...

But the truth is... Never will it ever be the same,

For you have lost while the unfortunate count their moments...

So it's best, you leave them in their sundry exasperations,

For if they really needed a fulcrum,

They would have provided you with,

All the aliments.

# I was Told

This year has been extraordinary for someone as ordinary as me...

I was told it couldn't be done;

A babe in hand would mean a lot of work,

I saw his toothless smile, and all I could say was...

Hello there, I have been blessed with an angel in disguise.

I was told It couldn't be done;

A career-driven by passion is only an illusion,

With a click of a button I sent a draft & all I could say was...

This is the beginning of a whole new start.

I was told it couldn't be done;

Long-distance relationships won't last that long,

I get a call from my love seas apart, and all We say is...

I love you so very much!

And all the three hearts warm up with a thousand light bulbs!

# PLAUSIBLE
# INTERPRETATIONS

# I Yearning and Seeking

## The Innocent

- **The Beauty of Beauty** - When it's difficult for us to come to terms with something, we often feel that innocence is bliss; however, this poem says otherwise.

- **Wild Child** - In the span of a day, we find ourselves feeling guilty when we succumb to our guilty pleasures and the chatter of our mind, this poem explores that.

- **Tears -** The poem talks about the pain one feels when you give more than you receive in a relationship.

- **It Feels As If** - the poem talks about heartbreak and betrayal by a loved one and the naiveness for having loved someone.

- **Why so Serious** - The clash of egos in a relationship, the back and forth of it often seems like a dance, this poem talks about learning to accept the circumstances you are in by not taking it too seriously.

- **Love** - The metaphor of dawn is used to express the aspect of infinity and new beginnings in the same relationship.

- **Seed to a Tree** - The poem talks about exercising maturity instead of resorting to a regressive child-like behaviour.

- **Strength Within** - This poem is for younglings to validate their fears and to help them find the light when they experience loneliness.

# The Philosopher

- **Phases** - The poem outlines the journey and the aspects of growth a homo sapiens experience.

- **The Catalyst** - Love is described as a form of a catalyst that changes you; however, it ends on a note where one feels lost, and love is only a form of yearning.

- **Meanings** - An attempt is made to empathize and give definitions to another's actions and needs in our own head, based on our own interpretations in an effort to reconcile.

- **Mirrors** - The poem speaks of how one projects one's feelings onto others and how we display or reverberate our own actions and thoughts, and so do others.

- **Something's** - Many times we come across circumstances where we feel that we were misguided and the disappointment and betrayal one feels is encompassed in the poem.

- **Fear** - The poem tries to capture the experience of fear after realizing some existential truths.

- **The Chord** - The poem talks about the confusion and dilemma that arises when two individuals who love one another are in disagreement. Their choices are tangent to each other, but they are still trying to make sense of it all while still longing for validation and connection.

- **Bones of Contention** - The poem indulges in the form of a self-dialogue in an attempt to defend one's Self from the rejection and blame one is subjected to. It finds resolution in forgiving the Self and letting go.

- **A Path Different** - The poem draws parallels between ethics and empathy.

- **Infinity** - This poem talks about a catch 22 situation. The space and time that exists when you think hard about making a particular decision that will alter the course of life for you. It seems like an infinity till you arrive at a conclusion.

- **Intensely Same** - There is no barometer for pain, we all feel it, and no one is greater or smaller, the poem reiterates this.

- **The Worship** - The poem talks about the healing process while recovering from C-PTSD. It encapsulates trauma, the coping mechanisms, memory flashbacks, the ruthless inner critic, dissociation and other aspects of C-PTSD while seeing the light through it all.

• **Bruises Black and Blue** - The poem tries to empathize with the reader's pain in an attempt to give hope in their darkest days.

• **Embers Red** - The concept and ritual of death are explored in this poem.

• **Now** - The poem talks about being mindful and living in the present, especially when you feel too overwhelmed with your own Self.

# The Explorer

- **Sky Life** - The shades of the sky is used as a metaphor to experience life.

- **Youth** - The poem describes the crossroads we encounter while deciding on a career as we take a step into a new role and stage of the human cycle.

- **A New Beginning** - A Fresh slate or a start accompanies with it regret as well as hope, the poem elucidates this,

- **Skin Deep** - It draws a parallel between sadness and happiness

- **Freedom -** The poem explores the aspects of the autonomous Self and practising detachment to pursue your goals.

- **A Poem** - A simple poem that talks about achieving one's dream.

- **Discover** - It talks about finding freedom together and an escape.

- **Whole** - Words are used in a minimalistic way to describe the merging of perspectives and diminishing of boundaries.

- **The Rose** - The poem inspired by the DaVinci Code book talks about the mysteries that are hidden in everyday life.

- **I Am** - A parallel is drawn between Nature and the Self yet again while experiencing a higher state of consciousness.

# II Connecting with Others

## The Orphan

- **Wonders Within** - The poem talks about the magic of serendipity and finding a soul mate by using mythical metaphors.

- **The Candescent Zephyr** - The poem speaks of quiet confidence while loving an introvert.

- **Killing Myself Softly** - It talks about toxic self-sacrifice in order to feel loved.

- **Driving Loneliness** - An attempt is made to make the reader find a course of action that would mitigate loneliness.

- **Sold my Soul** - We often know when some is playing games with us, knowingly, unknowingly we too go along with the flow however ultimately it runs its course, and you realize the price it has cost you after your ego is bruised.

- **See you Again** -Many time's relationships end on sour notes whether we had intended them to or not. Anguish builds up while we long for some closure, but it doesn't see the light of day. This poem gives an insight as to how a healthy closure would look like.

- **My Ally** - A light-hearted poem that urges for a sense of belonging.

# The Jester

- **Crush** - A few lines encompassing the fluttering of the heart when you have just developed a crush on someone.

- **Neon Sign** - The poem talks about making the first move and giving a signal hoping the other person recognizes it and does the same.

- **Forbidden Love** - The poem navigates the excitement that one may feel to chase an unavailable partner, however, in the end, making a choice that wouldn't lead to self-sabotage.

- **The Beauty and the Beast** - The poem uses the analogy of the story - Beauty and the Beast to talk about body consciousness and empathize with someone's perceived imperfections to make them feel beautiful inside and out.

- **The Mango Tree** - A comparison is drawn between mature but egotistical love and that of childhood. An attempt is made to portray that breakups and heartaches need not be so intense or ruthless.

- **Learning to Fly** - The poem talks about going easy on yourself, especially the times when you are ridden with the guilt of not doing enough.

- **A Daydream** -As the name suggests, it talks about a daydream and allowing yourself to escape to a space where you can just be.

- **Chocolates** - Sweet moments shared with a loved one are savoured in this poem.

# The Lover

- **The Beauty of a Soul** - This poem describes that phase of the relationship when you are unsure and still learning to trust someone.

- **Losing** - The poem talks about reminiscing of someone you were fond of.

- **A Promise** - The poem takes a more utopian form in processing one's love.

- **Till Death Do Me Apart** - The poem verbalizes the apprehension of longing and separation a lover feels knowing that the person they hold dear is soon going to leave.

- **Jhelum** - The title was inspired by a river of Kashmir and expresses a lover's longing for her loved one to come back home soon.

- **Longing** - The yearning and longing for being loved are expressed in this poem.

- **Hoping No More** - Sometimes even going through a day can seem like a task when you're waiting for a soulmate to turn up; for that Mills & Boon story to come alive and finally realizing that it won't.

- **Caress my Soul** - The poem talks about the need for a sense of safety and security from a loved one amid challenging circumstances.

- **Trying Not to Try** - Many times, in trying to do the right thing and avoid others' disappointment, our own personal boundaries are violated, and the self-starts to erode. It's this anguish that the poem describes.

- **Loops** - The poem talks about establishing boundaries while coming out of a co-dependent relationship. The way it might backfire when faced with criticism by others as well as our own selves.

- **Greener Someday** - The poem talks about loving and being in a relationship with someone who doesn't love you back.

- **A Thought** - The only poem in Hindi, it expresses the disdain felt from a loved one, and an attempt is made to melt their heart to fall in love again by urging them to acknowledge the pain they have inflicted.

- **The Pole Star** - The poems express the frustration that arises when you bequeath too much in a relationship, and the anticipation one has that a loved one would love you and behave as per your expectations.

- **No More** - The phase that comes after the end of a relationship, where all communication ceases is spoken about in this poem.

- **Buddy** - Many a time taking a step back could save a potential relationship from complete disintegration. In slang terms, the poem talks about friend-zoning someone.

- **By your Side** - The poem assertively brings forth the need to have honesty and a healthy balance of reciprocity in a relationship.

- **Surrender** - The poem speaks of the emotional and psychological freedom attained after coming to terms with a painful betrayal.

- **Sweet dreams** - The poem talks about how dreams can metamorphose the fulfilment of unmet needs and desires.

# III Providing Order

## The Altruist

- **The Cuddle** - The musings of a soon to be Mother are shared in this poem and all the things she wants her unborn child to know. Hoping it serves as a time capsule for the child to understand and navigate the life they soon are about to experience.

- **The Midnight Prose** - A New Year's Eve spent alone and the anguish and hope to connect with others and explore more to life is what inspired the poem.

- **The Little Moongusie** - The poem explores the experiences of a new mother.

- **Mother's Day** - The poem is a small ode to a caregiver defining their heart and praising their selfless Nature.

- **The Doctor** - The poem talks about a mother's role as a healer.

- **My Little Elf** - The poem expresses the awe and observation a sibling has for their baby brother or sister.

- **Bruvver** - A poem Dedicated by an older sister to her young brother.

- **Special Bond** - The poem speaks of the platonic love a fan has for the noteworthy figure they admire and idolize.

- **I Wish** - A heartfelt poem wishing grace for a loved one.

- **I Love You** -A lover's gratitude towards the person who has been their strength and been there through thick and thin is expressed in this poem.

- **Falling** - The poem appreciates the acts of kindness of a loved one and the beginning of when one's heart melts.

- **Season of Winter** - The metaphor of winter is used to describe hardships that may come in a relationship, and the firm will to weather all the storms.

- **The Second Sun** - Second chances are hard to come by; the poem talks about the humility involved in them and the power of shared sanguine memories of past events that help them happen.

- **A Story of You and Me** - The poem takes cognizance of the divine grace and the way we perceive it when we are at our weakest after experiencing loss

# The Ruler

- **The Lost Love** - The poem takes the perspective of a woman scorned in love.

- **Crater Half of the Moon** - The poem captures the dynamics of the fights that may ensue between a couple and how a woman can feel comforted when there is a storm raging within her, knowing that she is not at her best Self.

- **The Frenemy** - Sometimes our closest can be our worst enemies as they disguise their true intentions by using tricks of manipulation. The poem unveils these aspects and tells us what to do about it.

- **Truth or Dare** - The poem talks about seducing and challenging the other person.

- **The Hurricane** - The poem talks about taking control of one's own sexuality and expressing it and owning it for yourself without the weakness and jealousy attached to it.

- **The Giant** - When faced with heartbreak, we often find it challenging to rise up again, this poem, on the contrary, elucidates the confidence that one can learn to love again better and more significantly.

# The Artist

- **Pencil** - The form of a pencil is personified, and the process of artistic creation is explored.

- **Yin and Yang** - The poem describes an artist and the creation of their artwork from an observer's point of view. It further delves into the symbolism of love, hope, and life.

- **The Sonnet** - The poem elucidates the frustration and the catharsis that accompanies the process of writing.

- **World of my Own** - While creating something beautiful, you may get entangled in the web of overt rationality in the form of obsessive thinking and self-doubt. The poem beckons you to find solace in such times in your heart and trust yourself.

- **Clarity** - The poem speaks of cultivating focus and dedication.

- **A Dream** - Being stonewalled by someone even when you still are longing for them can create a lot of turmoil. The poem speaks of coming to terms with the situation and taking the onus to create something worthwhile out of it. It likens it to the phenomenon of letting go, just like we let go of our dreams when we wake up and set realistic goals that would make us happy.

- **The Doppelgänger** - The poem talks about a sense of security a fantasy of the person you love may provide, primarily when it doesn't entail any of their negative qualities and they become the perfect partner that you hope for.

- **Potions** - Friendship comes in different permutations and combinations as per the liberty and convenience of the people involved.

- **Shadows** - The shadow is personified in an attempt to shun mediocrity that professes superficial and hypocritical dialogues and instead finds real value in the principles of humanity.

- **The Adventure** - The poem urges you to dive within as a form of adventure to explore yourself. It talks about creating an anchor within the mind when one is in the midst of chaos.

- **The Grit** - The poem beckons you to rise from the harsh realities of anxiety, negative voices, and trauma and convert it into something powerful through sheer indomitable Will.

# IV Leaving a Mark

## The Warrior

- **Emerald** - Inspired by the movie The Great Gatsby, it showcases the courage of love in a society where individuals can't be trusted.

- **Dream Again** - A reassuring poem to read when your dreams feel threatened.

- **Cold Feet** - A string of thoughts portrayed in the mind of someone who is about to get married.

- **Strings Attached** - We often succumb to relationships that are not right for us, this poem speaks of the realization of your real needs and accountability in relationships mounting to the fact that you deserve better.

- **The Cure** - This poem talks of a seemingly ordinary day seeding within it an extraordinary moment of having overcome a significant challenge akin to a cure. It also reflects the relief and apprehensions of facing challenges again.

- **The Change** - The poem speaks of how time and circumstances may change the dynamics of a relationship and the individuals themselves. How to traverse such tides and discover what it means to fall in love with change.

- **The Blue Whale** - The poem talks of hope in the time of despair. Reminding one that pain is not a punishment but a signal to take cognizance of circumstances and churn it into your greatest strength.

- **The Demon Vanquished** - The poem cites an instance of having faced your perpetrator. The healing that has been done after the confrontation with your fears. The questions that arise, the strength you realize as you come to terms with the new reality and the awareness that sinks into you emotionally and psychologically.

- **The Waves** - The poem personifies the acts of self-sabotage and the urges to keep indulging in it. The way it tempts you but still finding the courage to break free of the pattern.

- **The Eclipse** - Liberating oneself from a toxic co-dependent relationship and walking out from their shadow into a more healthy way of living is the theme of the poem.

- **Birthday** - The poem speaks of the impression and imprints an individual as left on her and her belief that one day the world too would be able to see their potential.

- **Shimmering light** - The poem elicits to bring forth your strength when faced with tough decisions and choices and to assuage the fears of making a mistake.

# The Wizard

- **The Surf** - The poem narrates the positive psychological and emotional transformations a woman experiences after childbirth.

- **Words** - It talks about words yielding the power of a double-edged sword.

- **Eyes of Stone** - The poem speaks of the Will that is formed after a decision is made of not going back to a relationship which has turned sour.

- **The Fatal Flaw** - The poem speaks of a storm that rages within us when we are wild with anger and the destruction that is caused when we are at its mercy. When the realization dawns once the calm sets, it's almost too late. However, the hope still persists that we eventually learn to accept our innate natures and wish that someone would love us unconditionally despite it.

- **I Am Therefore I Think** - This poem talks about defending, rectifying and admitting a misunderstanding and taking accountability to set things right.

- **21 Days** - Written during the Coronavirus lockdown phase in the month of early April, it gives an insight into the happenings during that time.

- **The Making** - The poem outlines the mental process of how a vision starts to develop once you realize what it is that you are seeking.

# The Rebel

- **Land of my Own** - The poem speaks of the despair one feels for not having achieved a particular goal that was envisioned. The way circumstances unfolded tangent to your expectations.

- **Losing Myself** - The poem talks of the alienation we feel when our own values and mindsets do not match that of the others. Not being able to find individuals of similar wavelength even after attempts of trying to fit in makes one feel caged.

- **Still Nowhere** - The poem urges you to take cognizance of the prevalent gender biases and the apathy that arises once you realize that not much is being done for women's rights.

- **The Patriarch** - The poem speaks of the prevalent narcissism that exists in our social fabric and how it is perpetuated in the family unit. It speaks of the final resolution required for the woman to come out of her subservience and assert her dominance to survive.

- **Fairness** - When faced with harsh realities of life, one tends to introspect, the poem explores this.

- **Blessings and Curses** - Giving multiple analogies and using rhetorical questioning the poem urges you to reevaluate the things that you have been told and find new perspectives. It attempts to help you unlearn what you have learnt to gain fresh insights.

- **Into the Night** - the poem talks about the clarity gained once someone's real intentions come to light. The feelings of pain and betrayal that accompany the undressing of a mask and disguise to reveal a Machiavellian character.

- **Letting go** - The poem speaks of embracing the dark and coming to terms with the helplessness and hopelessness without fighting it. A surrender to powerlessness and the permission to allow yourself to feel the pain and sadness without trying too hard to find that glimmer of hope.

- **Just Once** - Using fair logic and earnestness, the poem shows that the concept of a soulmate or first love is overrated. It's entirely possible to fall in love again.

- **Confession** - The poem narrates the thoughts and dilemmas of a girl who has decided to make the first move.

- **Jungfrau** - The poem speaks of the biases and prejudices held with the concept of virginity and moving beyond it.

- **The Werewolf** - The poem entwines a lovers revenge and passion for bringing out the commonalities of both the emotions.

- **The Spine** - The poem personifies the human spine to represent courage and its importance, especially in circumstances when your own loved ones don't show any.

- **I was Told** - The lines showcase as to how society at large may discourage you, but you manage to prove them wrong and find your own way.

Printed in Great Britain
by Amazon